THE TALIBAN AND BEYOND
A Close Look at the Afghan Nightmare

S. Amjad Hussain

BWD Publishing

Perrysburg, OH

THE TALIBAN AND BEYOND
A Close Look at the Afghan Nightmare

S. Amjad Hussain

BWD Publishing
Perrysburg, OH

ISBN: 0-9710723-1-0

Published by BWD Publishing
320 Louisiana Ave
P O Box 602
Perrysburg, OH 43551
www.bwdpublishing.com
info@bwdpublishing.com

Printed and bound in the United States of America

Dedicated to

Dottie
friend, confidant and life partner
And to our children
Natasha, Waqaar and Osman

The most significant milestones in my journey through life

Also by S. Amjad Hussain

The Frontier Town of Peshawar
A brief history
1993, 1998, 1999

Yuk Shehre Arzoo (Urdu)

یک شہر آرزو

1995
(Winner of the Abasin Literary Gold Medal)

Of Home and Country
Journey of a Native Son
1998

Aalam Mein Intikhab-Peshawar (Urdu)

عالم میں انتخاب ۔ پشاور

1999

Matti Ka Qarz (Urdu)

مٹی کا قرض

2000

The First 150 Yars-
A History of The Academy of Medicine
of Toledo and Lucas County
1851- 2001
(in collaboration with Barbara Floyd and Vicki L. Kroll)
2001

دپیینے نه تینبة نیشة

There is no escape from the inevitable

Pushtu Proverb

Introduction

Afghanistan is an enigma that defies understanding. It is a land that even the native Afghans and its closest friends and neighbors have difficulty understanding. As one who was born and raised in the frontier town of Peshawar, just miles on the Pakistani side of the wild frontier, I too find it difficult to present a coherent account of the country.

The Afghans, particularly those in the Pushtun east and south of the country are extremely religious people. They practice an orthodox version of Islam that is interspersed with feudal tribal traditions. This combustible mix has often split them at the ethnic seams but has also helped them unite against a common, often foreign, enemy. The Afghans successfully defeated (with massive help and assistance from America, Saudi Arabia and Pakistan) a super power in the Soviet Union. But when left to their own designs, they sank into the depths of a brutal civil war.

The Taliban rose from the ashes of a devastated country and in a short period of six years captured 90 percent of the territory from various warlords, corrupt Mujahideen and an ineffectual and incompetent central government. To most outsiders, their success was   hard to explain. To the Taliban it was Allah's will. Armed with the holy writ, they went about projecting a face of Islam that is unfamiliar and unrecognizable to most Muslims.

But they went further. They considered themselves the inheritors of a true Islam and embarked upon exporting it to other Muslim countries. If an indigenous Islamic movement coming out of mosques and religious schools can achieve unprecedented success in Afghanistan, it can certainly lead the rest of the world toward the true path. Enter Osama bin Laden, and along the way, the pristine Islamic teachings of tolerance, acceptance and accommodation gave way to self-righteousness, militancy and brutality.

I had been a rather frequent visitor to Afghanistan prior to the deposition of King Zahir Shah in 1973. Kabul has always had a lure for us frontiersmen, in part because of shared history, cultural kinship and the bonds of Pushtu language. We felt more at home in Kabul than in many other places within our own country of Pakistan. But on my last trip to the country in the winter of 2000, Afghanistan had changed.

It has become a strange land that is ruled by an equally strange people. Though I profess to the same faith as the Taliban rulers and consider myself an observant Muslim, I could not relate to them. The religion that they preached and practiced was not the one I was born into and have practiced. It was a study in contrast.

I wondered about the views, opinions and aspirations of burqa-clad women in the bazaar of Kabul. I am no stranger to burqas. The women in my family wore them outside the home when I was growing up. But that was 50 years ago. The world is now more enlightened, and men in the Muslim world are sensitive to the aspirations of their twin halves as the women were called by Prophet Muhammad. At the dawn of 21st century, the reverse was true in Afghanistan.

I wrote my impressions of Afghanistan for the Toledo Blade as a special report series of front-page articles that were published in July, 2001. The Pittsburgh Post Gazette also carried an abbreviated version of the series. After the shocking events of Sept. 11, 2001, public interest in Osama bin Laden, the alleged mastermind behind the terrorist attacks, his protectors the Taliban and Afghanistan in general has caught the world attention. It was against this backdrop that I decided, with much prodding by many of my friends and my readers to expand those article into an easy-to-read short book.

There was a running joke among the Mujahideen in the 1980s about the itinerant journalists and writers who would come to Peshawar to "cover" the war in Afghanistan. They would venture into Afghanistan for few days and then write a book about their experience. The common refrain was the Persian *"seh roose, yuk kitab,"* literally "three days, one book." The much-hyped visit of CBS anchor Dan Rathers to Afghanistan during that period earned him the sneering title "Ganga Dan" by the media critics. When writing about Afghanistan, one has to be mindful of superficial generalities.

What you are about to read is not based on my few visits to Afghanistan but on cumulative observations of the country and its people spanning 50 years. And still, I consider myself quite inadequate to explain Afghanistan to my own satisfaction.

At the end of this book, I have included a number of related articles in an appendix. I wrote those articles in the 1980s and 1990s about the ongoing war in Afghanistan. I hope these articles would provide a useful backdrop against the current situation in Afghanistan.

Also included is an epilogue that brings the recent developments to the end of November 2001, the time this book was going to the printer.

A few acknowledgments are in order.

I am most grateful John Robinson Block co-publisher and editor-in-chief of the Blade and Ron Royhab, executive editor at the Blade for their encouragement in writing the original articles. Jack Lessenberry a journalism professor at the Wayne State University, Detroit, and the ombudsman for the Blade, helped edit the original series and reviewed the current manuscript. I am indebted to him for his encouragement and his insightful critique.

During the preparation of special report on the Taliban for the Blade, I had the pleasure of working with Roger Downing, an editor at the newspaper. Roger's insightful critique was of immense value to me. He and his very capable wife, September, have reviewed and edited the manuscript of this book. I can not thank them enough for a wonderful job.

Rhondia Black, the CEO of BWD Publishing, deserves my appreciation for her enthusiasm in getting the book published in record time.

Every Thursday evening for the past 25 years, I have joined a group of my five friends to play cards, tell stories and discuss any subject that happens to be on our minds. At times they have challenged me beyond my capacity and capability, and certainly beyond my endurance, with their questions and their comments. I am grateful for their company and their friendship. Thank you Munir Ahmad, Karim Zafar, Jim Adray, Naveed Ahmed and Bahu Shaikh.

Toledo, Ohio   S. Amjad Hussain
November 2001.   aghaji@buckeye-express.com

Contents

The Taliban and Beyond

A Close Look at the Afghan Nightmare

As a bright winter sun sets behind the snow-covered western mountains, Kabul slides into a tranquil darkness. Here and there on the street a few eating places cater to an occasional diner. The aroma of roasted meat from the sidewalk grills wafts through the neighborhood and permeates the evening air. On the dark hills in the distance a few lights twinkle with uncertainty. The eerie quietness is broken by the piercing call for prayers from a near by mosque. A sense of gloom hangs heavy on the city of Kabul as this once fabled city on the ancient Silk Road sinks in darkness in more ways than one.

Even to those who have been its guest, Afghanistan has become a strange and unfamiliar country. And it is getting stranger by the day. It is in constantly in the news for the weird and bizarre policies of its Taliban rulers. In 2000 the Taliban captured world attention for the destruction of ancient statues of Buddha in Bamiyan Valley in the northwest of the country. And now in the fall of 2001 they have triggered a de facto war between their impoverished country and the United States in the aftermath of the vicious terrorists attack on World Trade Center in New York and the Pentagon in Washington.

Who are the Taliban and how did they come to be the rulers of Afghanistan? Are they the fanatic zealots who have turned the clock back to the medieval times or the saviors of Afghanistan, who have brought the country out of the clutches of a bloody civil war? Or is it just one more convulsive upheaval in the long and fascinating history of Afghanistan? These and many more questions brought me to this once fabled city on the ancient Silk Route.

Experts say, with some justification, that it is impossible to understand Afghanistan and for that matter the Afghans. One cannot understand the present-day Afghanistan without looking at its tortured and often bloody history.

1

Afghanistan Through the Ages

Starting in 600 BC, the area comprising present day Afghanistan was successively ruled by the Acheamenian rulers of Iran, Alexander the Great of Macedonia and the Maurian kings of India. In 175 BC Demetrius established an Indo-Greek dynasty in parts of Afghanistan and India. Though all of them have left their mark on the region, none was more enduring and permanent than those left by the nomadic Kushan tribes of Central Asia.

In the beginning of the Christian era the Kushans established their vast Gandhara Empire in the present-day Afghanistan, most of northern Pakistan and parts of India, reaching in the east to China. The empire reached its zenith under King Kanishka whose benevolent rule and his love for art attracted pilgrims and artisans from as far away as Rome and China. The Buddhist Kushans also helped spread their religion beyond the borders of their empire. It was in that era that the giant Buddhas were carved in the mountain face in Bamiyan Valley. Long after the disintegration of Gandhara Empire in the 4th century, its imprint remained.

Advent of Islam in Afghanistan

The advent of Islam in Afghanistan is shrouded in mystery. Tribal folklore and oral history place the event in the later part of 7th century when Arabs conquered Persia and extended their influence to the western frontier of India. According to tribal folklore and oral history, an Arab missionary by the name of Khalid bin Abdullah settled down among the Pushtun tribes in the east and south of present-day Afghanistan and was responsible for converting the Buddhists tribes to Islam.

However some historians place the arrival of Islam around the 10th century. While Islam had reached Iran and Central Asia in relatively short time after its beginning in the Arabian Peninsula in the 7th century, the impenetrable Hindu Kush Mountains in the northwest of Afghanistan delayed its arrival in Afghanistan for another 200 years. By the 10th century, Islam had effectively replaced Buddhism in Afghanistan and adjacent areas of Pakistan.

Starting in the 10th century a string of Muslim dynasties, many of them from Central Asia, ruled Afghanistan. There were the Ghaznavids, the Ghorids, the Seljuk Turks and the Mongol Hordes. The latter dynasty under Genghis Khan in 1220 let loose a wave of destruction to retaliate the death of his grandson in a battle at Bamiyan, the site of the destroyed giant Buddhas. Ironically neither Genghis Khan nor one of the earlier Afghan kings, Mahmud of Ghazna, commonly known as the 'idol smasher,' caused any harm to the statues. Mahmud's 17 excursions into India were not for exporting the religion of Islam but to loot the rich temples of Hindu religion.

Next came the Central Asian Turks who established the Mogul dynasty and ruled India and occasionally Afghanistan for the next 200 years. As the borders of the Mogul Empire shrunk, the restive Afghan tribes rebelled against them and for another two centuries, kings from the various Afghan tribes maintained an uneasy hold on the country. It is interesting to note that all Afghan kings came from the dominant Pushtun tribes from the east and south of the country. They ruled with the help of their own tribes with an un-easy coalition with the Uzbeks, Tajiks and Hazaras in the north and northwest of the country.

It was in the 19th century that Great Britain and czarist Russia vied for influence in Afghanistan. Rudyard Kipling, the irrepressible chronicler of the British colonial era, wrote about the menace of Russian expansion in his short story 'Mutiny of the Mavericks':

> *Listen in the north my boys, there is trouble in the wind;*
> *Tamp o' Cossack hooves in front, grey great coat behind,*
> *Trouble on the Frontier of most amzin' kind,*
> *Trouble on the waters of the Oxus!*

By this time in the early part of 19th century the British had switched their roles in India from traders to administrators of large areas of India in the south and east of the subcontinent. The East India Company was now ruling India in the name of the British monarch. Fearful of Russian invasion of India through the northern Pamir Mountains of Afghanistan, the British decided to have a visible presence in Kabul. In time, 150 years to be precise, the British would realize that it would have been impossible for the Russians to invade India through the impenetrable Pamir Mountains. But the policies set in motion to prevent such eventuality led the British, in the span of 70 years, to fight three wars with the Afghans. They lost all three.

The first Afghan war was fought in 1840 when the Afghan king Dost Muhammad Khan sought the help of British East India Company to regain control of Peshawar Valley from the Sikhs. The Sikhs had wrestled control of the strategic Peshawar Valley from the Afghans after a fiercely fought battle on the western bank of the Indus River.

By 1826 the Sikh flag flew over the Khyber Pass. While the British would have liked to get a foothold in Kabul, a treaty of non-interference with the Sikhs prevented them from helping the king. In another 50 years the British would set aside that treaty, grab the Punjab from Sikhs and march on to Peshawar.

But at the time they did not want to disturb the Sikhs and instead decided to get rid of Dost Muhammad Khan and restore Shah Shujah on the Kabul throne. In the shifting sands of Afghan tribal loyalties Shah Shujah had earlier been cast away in favor of Dost Muhammad and was now living in exile in India.

A three-pronged British expeditionary force, the army of the Indus, invaded Afghanistan and restored Shah Shujah to the throne. Having accomplished their immediate goal, the British settled down to a comfortable life in Kabul. This proved to be a lull before the storm. Within a year the tribes revolted against the king and his foreign protectors over reduction in subsidies that the British had promised. With Kabul up in flames, the British made a hurried retreat from Kabul for Jalalabad. Those who survived periodic attacks by the pursuing tribesmen, succumbed to bitter cold and starvation. The contingent of 4,500 men, women and children perished in the wasteland between Kabul and Jalalabad. The sole survivor was one Dr. William Brydon, a medical officer with the British army, who staggered on horseback in the British camp in Jalalabad to tell the story. The British would pay a heavy price again in 1880 and then in 1919 in the subsequent two wars for their ill conceived excursions into a hostile land.

The Indo-Afghan border has always been fuzzy, unclear and wild. For Afghans the boundary of their country has always been the Indus

River, 80 miles east of the Khyber Pass. With historic justification they have also claimed a wide swath of tribal territory the runs north-south from Chitral in the north to Wazirstan in the south and including Dir, Bajaur and Swat as well as the Valleys of Peshawar and Kurram. Before the westward expansion of the Sikh kingdom of Punjab in 1826, the city of Peshawar had served as winter capital of the Afghan kings.

Toward the latter part of 19th century, the British, still preoccupied with the menace of southward expansion of the czarist Russia started to consolidate their hold on the disputed tribal territory that Afghanistan had always claimed. In a dispatch to the British in 1892, an Afghan king, King Abdur Rahman protested the 'nibbling away of (his) territory' by the British and divided the tribes along a fictitious geographic line. In1893 Sir Mortimer Durand, the British foreign secretary visited Kabul and convinced the king to accept a boundary demarcation drawn by them. Under duress and with promises of large subsidies the king capitulated and ceded large chunks of Afghan territory to British India. The new boundary, the Durand Line, sliced through the Pushtun tribes and divided them along a new imaginary border that had no historic validity. By drawing the border 80 miles west of the Indus River the British effectively neutralized Afghanistan's historic claims on Peshawar as well as the historic and strategic Khyber Pass. As long as British ruled India the validity of the Durand Line was not in dispute. After creation of Pakistan in western parts of British India, Afghanistan demanded the return of areas east of the Durand Line including their winter capital, Peshawar. Afghanistan claim for the return of ceded territory continued to be the main reason for bad relations between Afghanistan and Pakistan until the Soviet invasion of Afghanistan in 1979.

Before the partition of British India in 1947, people in the North West Frontier Province along the Afghan border decided, in a referendum, to join Pakistan. Whereas a great majority in the province was in support of the creation of Pakistan, the tribal population straddling the Durand Line was less than enthusiastic. After the partition, both Pakistan and Afghanistan pursued a policy of appeasement toward the tribes on the Pakistan side of the Durand Line. The tribes exploited this to the fullest of their advantage. They remained loyal to nobody but them-selves while all the time pledging allegiance to Pakistan. In years to come, the conflicting loyalties on the part of Pushtun tribes and Paki-stan's effort at placating the tribes would extract a heavy price from Pakistan. The country would be drawn into regional conflicts that would not be of its own making or liking.

The demarcation of a border between British India and Afghanistan created another geographic anomaly as well. In a concession to King Abdur Rahman, the British allowed the king to keep a narrow strip of land in the north as a buffer between British India and czarist Russia. This finger like northeastern projection of Afghanistan called the Wakhan corridor touches China in its most eastern point.

Most Afghan kings, while not fighting foreign invaders, had to fight the forces of orthodoxy within their borders. In a difficult balancing act they treaded the fine line between modernity and orthodox reli-gious traditions. Not many have succeeded and quite a few lost their neck for over stepping that boundary. The story of King Amanullah Khan and his successor illustrates this point rather well and has the echoes of the present rise of the Taliban.

Son of the Water Carrier
Bacha Saqao - An Early Talib

The reformist king Amanullah Khan was determined to bring his country into the modern age. But his ideas of modernity were too radical and the pace too fast. The powerful mullahs labeled him an infidel and instigated people to rise against his rule. In late 1928 as the country sank into a civil war, a Tajik army deserter Habibullah Khan, a desperado and folk hero who became known as Bacha Saqao, literally "the son of the water carrier" gathered support and marched on Kabul. As Amanullah Khan made a hurried exit from the country, Bacha Saqao proclaimed himself the king. He let loose a reign of terror, closed all modern schools, pushed women back into the homes, kicked out foreign advisors and repealed laws against polygamy. He also sacked libraries, palaces and museums. He disbanded the ministries of justice and education as he considered them to be infringements on the power of the religious establishment. As it happened during the Taliban, the mullahs were handed over those functions. He lasted nine months before he was killed.

After going through the tyrannical rule of Bacha Saqao, a semblance of normalcy returned to the country in 1929 when the *Loya Jirga* or the grand assembly of tribal elders selected a Pushtun leader, Nadir Khan, as their king. Like Amanullah Khan who now lived in exile in Zurich, Switzerland, Nadir Khan was an enlightened person. He re-started the painful process of bringing Afghanistan out of its feudal past by opening new schools, a literary academy, a military college, a medical school and sent young Afghan boys and girls, to study abroad. He also introduced a bicameral legislature in the country. Tribal rivalry and militant orthodoxy joined hands to oppose his reforms. Within four years of his rule, he was assassinated.

His son Zahir Shah, the last of the Afghan kings, continued his father's policy of cautious reforms. Despite poverty and feudal tribal structure, Afghanistan under King Zahir Shah made steady and significant progress. He instituted compulsory education, opened state-of-the-art hospitals and sent young men and women to study abroad. In an artful international balancing act of non-alignment, he played the Soviet Union, the United States and Great Britain to the benefit of his country. Kabul became a sophisticated and cosmopolitan city during his reign.

In 1973, after 40 years of peaceful and progressive reign, the king was deposed by his cousin and Prime Minister Sardar Daud Khan, who packed the king off to Rome to live out his life in exile. The coup against King Zahir Shah was the start of the latest upheaval in Afghan history. In a brief period of six years, the former Soviet Union engineered three bloody coups and countercoups and paved the way for the invasion of Afghanistan in 1979.

2

The Long Nightmare of Soviet Occupation
1979-89

The lessons of Afghan history must have been lost on the communist rulers in the Kremlin when they decided to invade Afghanistan in 1979. Of all the people in the world, the Russians should have known from their long and often uneasy relations with their southern neighbors, that Afghans do not take kindly to outsiders coming into their country.

Soon after the Soviet invasion, a rag-tag group of freedom fighters, the Mujahideen, took up arms against the invaders. It was a shaky and uncertain start. But the movement grew, and in the next two years, the Soviets were engaged on many fronts by 10 different groups of Mujahideen. Some of the Mujahideen leaders were activists from Kabul University where they had led demonstrations and protests against the reformist King Zahir Shah, and later against the Soviet supported Afghan governments. Many of these leaders who had been in exile in the Middle East returned to Afghanistan to join the holy war.

Given the superior firepower of the Soviet Union, it would have been a no-win situation for the Mujahideen, who had nothing but antiquated small arms at their disposal, had it not been for massive support from the United States and several Arab states. In this situation, America and the West saw an unprecedented opportunity to humiliate an enemy who had done them so much harm in Vietnam. Ronald Reagan threw his full support behind the Mujahideen. The oil rich countries of Saudi Arabia and of the Persian Gulf also joined in the effort of the "believers" against the infidel Soviets. Pakistan became the front-line state in this effort, with money, arms and ammunition starting to flow to the Mujahideen across its borders. Pakistan would bear the brunt for its support of the war effort and would continue to pay a high price for its involvement for years after the last Soviet soldier was gone.

Though the West did not commit forces in Afghanistan, thousands of Muslim youth from around the world answered the call for *jihad*. At the height of war in the mid-1980s, a staggering 35,000 outsiders were fighting the Soviet forces in Afghanistan. Most of these fighters came from the Arab countries, but a good number came from Pakistan, Indonesia, the Philippines and Malaysia. The now notorious Osama bin Laden from Saudi Arabia was one such person who was attracted to the holy war against the Soviets and became part of that effort. He not only gave generously for the effort but fought alongside the Mujahideen. Ironically, the CIA trained him in one of its training camps in Pakistan. After the war, these foreign mercenaries would become a constant source of trouble for the moderate Arab and Muslim countries in the world. Osama bin Laden would change his focus from fighting the Soviet infidels to fighting the very benefactor, the United States, who had helped win the war.

It is often said that the war in Afghanistan was brought to its conclusion not as much by the tenacity of the Mujahideen or the massive military support from the United States, but by the introduction of highly portable stinger ground-to-air missiles. By the late 1980s, the war in Afghanistan was starting to show evidence of a stalemate. The Soviets controlled the cities whereas the Mujahideen controlled the countryside. The stingers tipped the balance in favor of the Mujahideen for now they had a weapon to match the Soviets' helicopter gunships. After the war, the United States military bought back some of the missiles, but many of them made their way to the Middle East and quite a few are reputed to be in the arsenal of the Taliban.

The war in Afghanistan was costly. The United States and the Western allies spent $5 billion, whereas Saudi Arabia and the Gulf States gave another $5 billion for the effort. It cost the Soviet Union $5 billion and thousands of casualties.

The end of war in Afghanistan was also the beginning of the end of the Soviet Union and the liberation of the East Europe and Central Asia from Soviet control. The victory however came at a price for Afghanistan. An already poor country was left devastated with 1 million dead and 6 million, one-fourth of its population, uprooted and forced to live in refugee camps in Iran and Pakistan.

The Civil War

True to their tribal history, once the Soviet forces left, the Mujahideen took on each other for control of the country. As the country sank into anarchy, Afghanistan split into small fiefdoms where each warlord controlled the passage of goods and travelers through his territory. Trade in illicit drugs, kidnapping for ransom and general lawlessness became the norm. To move goods over short distances the traders were forced to pay exorbitant sums in bribes and tributes. The traditional trade routes that connected Pakistan to Central Asia's markets all but shut down. The cultivation of poppy increased to the point where by the early-1990s Afghanistan became the main source of heroin to the West.

The Mujahideen and their warlords looted an already impoverished country by hauling off and selling telephone poles, wires, and equipment from factories and vehicles. Even the capital Kabul became a divided city where different factions controlled different parts of the city.

The United States and other Western countries have been rightly criticized for walking away from Afghanistan once their immediate

These two cartoons by the pre-eminent Pakistani cartoonist Muhammad Zahoor underscore the Mujahideen's role in the devastation of Kabul Left to their own designs after the defeat of the Soviet Union, the Mujahideen took on each other and sank the country into a bloody civil war.
These cartoons were published in 1992 in the Pakistani newspaper The Frontier Post and are reproduced with the permission of the artist.

objectives of defeating the Soviet Union were realized. What the West should have done was to infuse massive economic help to rebuild the country, which in turn would have led to nation building. Instead the Afghans were left to sort out things themselves that at the time they were totally incapable of doing.

The United Nations and Pakistan however tried very hard to get various Mujahideen factions to agree on a power sharing formula including all the ethnic groups. They tried to have the seven main religious parties, as well as the three secular leaning parties to come together for a unity government. There were many accords reached and the parties swore on the Qura'n to abide by them. Every one was broken in due course.

In the spring of 1992 there was yet another attempt by Pakistan to

force an agreement between the parties. While most of the Afghan leaders had gathered in the Governors House in Peshawar at the invitation of the then Pakistani prime minister Nawaz Sharif, two prominent leaders were conspicuously missing from the gathering: Gulbadeen Hikmatyar, the Pushtun leader of one of the main groups, mobilized his troops and headed for Kabul. Ahmad Shah Massoud, the charismatic Lion of Panjsher, stood guard on the northern fringes of the capital. As the remaining Afghan leaders huddled in Peshawar, the two archenemies waited at the gates of Kabul to strike the city and at each other. Finally, a 50-member interim council under the presidency of Sebghetullah Mojadedi, a moderate religious scholar, was formed. Both absentee leaders were given key portfolios: Hikmatyar was appointed prime minister and Massoud the defense minister. The final draft of the agreement had hardly been signed before the opposing forces entered Kabul and captured key installations. A fierce and bloody battle was fought between the rivals, and Massoud was able to remove Hikmatyar from the capital. Hikmatyar dug in a few miles south of the city and in the coming year would contribute to the destruction of the capital through random shellings of the city.

Even when the interim government did arrive in Kabul, the fighting between the forces of defense minister and the prime minister continued to the detriment of the hapless population. Where as the capital had emerged unscathed from the Soviet occupation, it was now subjected to unprecedented devastation and destruction at the hands of Afghans themselves. As the civil society broke down, an anarchy reigned in the capital. The saviors of Afghanistan had turned into looters and killers of their own people.

The Turning Point

In the southern city of Kandahar, things were no different. In the spring of 1994 a local commander abducted two girls, had their heads shaved and repeatedly raped them. The people had reached their breaking point. A local village mullah and teacher by the name of Muhammad Omar gathered 30 students from his religious school, and with 16 rifles between them, attacked the stronghold of the commander. They released the girls and then hanged the culprit from the barrel of a tank. Thus the one eyed cleric, an Afghan veteran, became a modern day Robin Hood for the poor and helpless people who had no recourse to the tyranny of the warlords. That watershed was the beginning of many more such incidents. Mullah Omar asked nothing in return but urged the establishment of a just Islamic order.

This led the Taliban, the students and teachers from *madrassas*, the religious schools, to organize and assert their authority in the whole Kandahar region. They restored law, disarmed the heavily armed populace and opened roads for free movement of people and goods. While the rest of the country continued to slide into the quagmire of anarchy, the Kandahar region was at peace.

3

Who Are the Taliban?

Literally meaning the seekers of knowledge, in this case religious knowledge, Taliban are the students and graduates from *madrassas* in Afghanistan and Pakistan. To understand their origin and their philosophy one needs to go back 200 years to the colonial era and the effect that period had on Muslim psyche.

During colonial rule, many reformist movements sprang up in the Muslim and Arab world to protect Muslim identity from what was thought to be the corrupting influences of Western culture. These movements were led, in different parts of the world, by diverse individuals; in the Arabian Peninsula by Muhammad Ibn Abd al-Wahhab (1703-1791), In Iran and Afghanistan by Jalal ad-Din al-Afghani (1839-1897), in Egypt by Muhammad Abduh (1849-1905) and in the Indian subcontinent by a number of Muslim scholars in the city of Deoband in the mid 19th century. While these revival movements and many others with the same purpose differed slightly in their interpretation of Islam, their underlying philosophy remained the revival of their faith to its simple and pristine roots that lay in 7th century Arabia.

Two of these movements are pertinent to the emergence of the Taliban movement and need some elaboration.

Wahhabism was a purely religious movement that helped Ibn Saud, the founder of the present day Saudi Arabi; subdue diverse tribes into a Saudi nation. The powerful religious establishment let the Ibn Saud family run the country as long as their rule was based on Wahhabi interpretation of Islam. Their interpretation strips the religion of all cultural and ethnic trappings to a simple, spartan and a bit harsh version. In Saudi Arabia criminals are dealt with swiftly and harshly, murderers are beheaded in public, women are required to wear a veil and a vigilant religious police makes sure men attend the mosques for obligatory prayers and observe dawn to dusk fasting during the month of Ramadan.

When oil rich Saudi Arabia started helping socio-religious causes and religious institutions in Muslim countries, it also started exporting its brand of Wahhabi Islam to those countries. During the war against the Soviet Union, the Mujahideen were recipient of not only petro dollars but of the Wahhabi ideology as well.

The Taliban's underlying philosophy however is deeply rooted in the 19th century Deobandi movement that started in the aftermath of the Indian Mutiny in 1857. At the time, many Muslim religious leaders realized that the British blamed Muslims for the mutiny and directed its retaliation against them. They believed it was because they had ignored the teachings of their religion that they were humiliated. It was only by getting back to the essence of their religion that Muslims would be able to preserve their religious heritage and progress in the world.

The Muslim *ulema*, the religious scholars, started a *madrassa* in the city of Deoband in India to reinculcate religious values in the Muslim youth and to counter the trend toward Western education. The Deobandis, as the followers of that *madrassa* are called, set up schools all over India that attracted a large number of Muslim youth from all across India and Afghanistan. Their curriculum then, as now, is based on traditional commentaries on the Qura'n, Hadith (the sayings of Prophet Muhammad) and texts on logic and Islamic jurisprudence. Arabic, the language of the Qura'n, is the only language taught in these schools. There are no courses in sciences, social studies or humanities.

It is interesting to note that just about the same time another reformist by name of Seyyed Ahmad Khan, later Sir Seyyed, started a school that took the opposite view. He emphasized the need for modern education along with religious education. This school would later grow into Aligarh Muslim University and would be a model for similar schools throughout the subcontinent. Whereas the Deobandi schools produced religious leaders and religious scholars, the Aligarh type of schools produced civil servants, politicians and professional. These two opposing education systems have remained on parallel tracks.

The underlying philosophy of most *madrassas* is *taqlid* or the acceptance of the old religious traditions and interpretations and not *ijtehad* or innovation in religious interpretation. While the medieval curriculum gives the students of these schools a sense of continuity and comfort, it effectively rules out any accommodation with modernity. The Taliban however have extended Deobandi interpretations to the extreme especially in the areas of women's role in the society and their negative attitude toward Shia Muslims. In time the rigid Deobandi philosophy spawned a number of anti-Shia movements in Pakistan that have wrecked havoc with the civil society and has plunged the country into communal blood letting in the past two decades.

For most graduates of *madrassa*, and many others of similar persuasion, history begins with the advent of Islam. Nothing existed before and even if something did exist, it is of no consequence. Their model of the Islamic State is from the times of the Prophet and the four Caliphs. While they are quick to claim the noble legacy of that period they fall short of the tolerance and acceptance of others that was preached by the Prophet and was the hallmark of that era.

In the 1980s, when Pakistan was under the military rule of Zia-ul-Haq, the number of *madrassas* proliferated in that country. Zia, in order to perpetuate his rule needed the support of Pakistani religious parties. During his campaign to "Islamize" the country, he channeled large sums of money to help establish such schools. Where as in 1972 there were only 900 *madrassas* in Pakistan, by the time Zia died in 1988, their numbers had jumped to 8,000 registered schools and 25,000 unregistered schools. As the state run education system became more inefficient and overcrowded, boys from poor families flocked to these schools to get some semblance of education. A great number of these students were from Afghan refugee camps in Pakistan.

Pakistani-Saudi-US Axis

As Pakistan's dream of access to the consumer markets of Central Asia through a pliant and peaceful Afghanistan vanished in the bloody chaos of the Afghan civil war, the Taliban emerged on the scene with their stunning victories in Kandahar region. Could the Taliban be the answer, the leaders in Islamabad wondered, to Afghanistan's never ending nightmare and a safe and secure trade route to Central Asia?

In the spring of 1995 Benazir Bhutto's interior Minister Naseerullah Babar, a retired army general, led a convoy of trucks carrying trade goods from southern Pakistani city of Quetta to the former Soviet republic of Turkmenistan, passing through the Afghan cities of Kandahar and Herat. Surprisingly, the U.S. envoy to Pakistan, John Monjo, was part of this motorized caravan over some of the world's oldest trade routes.

A Pakistani-Saudi-U.S. axis was in the making against the warring Mujahideen. In a dramatic shift of policy the then Pakistani Prime Minister Benazir Bhutto with the full backing of the United States decided to ditch the Mujahideen in favor of the Taliban. It was a calculated move on the part of Pakistan. Pakistan would get a pliable government in Afghanistan, would have an easy access to Central Asian markets, would be able to pacify Pakistani religious political parties and would be able to please Pushtun tribes living on the Pakistani side of the Durand Line. In time all those hopes were dashed because of single-minded zealotry of the Taliban. As the Taliban consolidated their hold on the country, the Mujahideen leaders such as Gulbadeen Hikmatyar went into exile. The others joined forces and formed the Northern Alliance to continue fighting the Taliban in the north of the country.

The Taliban are literally the orphans of the Afghanistan war. Most of them grew up in Afghan refugee camps in Pakistan. They knew Afghanistan but from a distance and that too through the prism of Islamic fundamentalism. In the *madrassas* they learned nothing about their own history except for the recent war of liberation. For them the *jihad* against the tyranny of warlords and the Mujahideen took on a new meaning that gave them a purpose as well as a possible future.

From their success in the Kandahar region and buoyed by the support of Pakistan and Saudi Arabia and with the tacit approval of the United

23

States, the Taliban started their sweep to conquer the entire country including the capital, Kabul.

4

The Emergence of the Supreme Leader

In the spring of 1996, 1,200 mullahs, mostly ethnic Pushtuns, gathered in Kandahar to decide the form of their future government. Even though there was some dissent among their ranks the majority wanted to install Mullah Muhammad Omar, the cleric who had started the movement by rescuing the kidnapped girls in Kandahar.

Mullah Muhammad Omar, a Ghilzai Pushtun, was born in a landless family about 1959 in Nodeh village near Kandahar. After his father's death in the late-1970s, he moved his family to Singesar village in the Mewand district of Kandahar. There he became the village mullah and opened a *madrassa* for village children. He did not take part in the *jihad* against the Soviets but took up arms against the communist government of Najibullah after the withdrawal of Soviet troops. For four years between 1989 and 1992 he was a fighter in the Hizb-e-Islami faction of the Mujahideen. During that time, he lost his right eye to a shrapnel wound and was wounded three other times. After the fall of Najibullah, Mullah Omar returned to his village to lead his congregation and to teach in the *madrassa* and settled down to a simple life with his three wives, five children and an extended family.

He would have remained an obscure Afghan mullah, not even a minor footnote in Afghan history, had it not been for the inhumane treatment of his people at the hand of the same Mujahideen that he had helped to defeat Najibullah.

Initially the 37-year-old mullah was reluctant to go along with the idea but relented under pressure. In a brilliant ploy to gain unanimous support he appeared before the gathering wearing a robe attributed to Prophet Muhammad. The assembled mullahs took allegiance to him and elected him Amir-ul-Momineen or the Commander of the Faithful. The title, not used in the past 1,400 years of Islamic history, has the implication that the holder speaks for all Muslims irrespective of where they live.

Years later he gave a simple explanation for the rise of the Taliban to Pakistani journalist Rahimullah Yusafzai during a rare interview: "We took arms to achieve the aims of the Afghan *jihad* and save our people from further suffering at the hands of the so called Mujahideen. We have complete faith in God Almighty. We never forgot that. He can bless us with victory or plunge us into defeat."

It is interesting to note that a good number of the Taliban were not in favor of putting themselves at the helm of the country. They wanted to clean the country of warlords and corrupt Mujahideen leaders, hand over the affairs to capable people and go back to their *madrassas*. But as they continued to sweep the country and saw how the ordinary Afghans welcomed them, they realized the opportunity to bring about an Islamic order that had eluded the mullahs throughout their history.

It took the Taliban another six months to capture Kabul and unify most of the country under their rule. Their spectacular success was universally welcomed including the United States. In a public statement, the State Department saw nothing objectionable in the fall of Kabul to the Taliban. Previously, at the time of the rise of the Taliban, Zbigniew Brezezinski, the former National Security advisor in the Carter administration had said about the Taliban: "What is more important in the world view of history? The Taliban or the fall of the Soviet Empire? A few stirred up Muslims or the liberation of Central Europe and the end of the Cold War?"

Upon entering Kabul, the Taliban attacked the U.N. compound where Najibullah, the last communist leader of the country, lived under U.N. protection during the Mujahideen government of Burhanuddin Rabbani. Despite prior assurances, Najibullah, his brother and many of his colleagues were summarily executed and their bodies strung in the bazaar for days.

Initially the people, tired of anarchy and lawlessness, welcomed the Taliban as God-sent holy knights in shining armor. The Taliban restored law and order and disarmed a heavily armed population. They also enforced a strict version of Sharia, or the Islamic law, that allows no room for argument or discussion. They banned music, closed girls' schools, forbade women to work outside the home, ordered every male to grow a beard and instituted public executions for murderers and cutting off the hands of habitual thieves.

The Taliban are an anathema not only to non-Muslims but also to many Muslims.

5

The 'Taliban University'

Before embarking on my journey to Kabul, I took a side trip in the Pakistani hinterland to visit a *madrassa*. Almost one third of the current Taliban leadership was educated in that one particular school. Jaamia Haqqania, as the school is called, is the epicenter of the Taliban philosophy and the spiritual center of gravity for the Taliban leadership.

The sprawling complex of Jaamia Haqqania is located at Akora Khattak on the Grand Trunk Road about 30 miles west of Peshawar. This dusty little town is the birth place of a Khushal Khan Khattak, an 18th-century poet Pushtun nationalist poet who wrote stirring poetry against the Mughal rulers and ironically against the tyranny of religious leaders.

Moulana Abdul Haq, a renowned religious scholar and the father of the current rector, started the school soon after the creation of Pakistan in 1947. Since its inception the school has set standards for religious education in Pakistan and has steadily grown in stature. The present sprawling complex consists of separate buildings for various departments and has 11 hostels. One hostel is reserved for foreign students from the Central Asian republics of Uzbekistan, Kazakhstan, Tajikistan and Kirgizstan and other Muslim countries. Pakistani students are mostly from the lower middle-class and poor families. Because of school's close association with the Taliban, a degree from this school is a sure ticket to a choice job in the Taliban government or in the

Moulana Sami-ul-Haq Spiritual mentor to the Taliban (Rector of Haqqania school near Peshawar, Pakistan)

mushrooming fundamentalist Islamic movements in Pakistan. The foreign students and a great many Pakistani students come to this dusty corner of Pakistan to become part of the Islamic renaissance as portrayed by the Taliban.

A few months before my visit, the New York Times Magazine had published a cover story on the school. The provocatively titled story "The Jihad University" had showed the school in rather poor light. At the time of my visit, the school officials were still angry and disappointed about the story and a bit paranoid about foreign reporters partaking of their open arm policy and their hospitality but not getting the story right. Fortunately a shared religion, my frontier background and my proficiency in Pushtu language were more than enough to get me a rare interview with the rector.

Moulana Sami-ul-Haq, the rector, is a cleric in his 50s with henna-dyed blazing red beard, a green turban and penetrating eyes. He is very articulate, extremely self-confidant and gracious. He wears many hats. Apart from running the school, he is the head of the Jamiat-e Ulamai-Islam, a religious political party, has taken a lead to bring major religious parties on one platform and heads a nationwide association of religious schools. He has also served in the Pakistan Senate in Islamabad before the military coup in 1999.

From Pakistani standards the school is impressive not as much for the brick and mortar but for its rigorous curriculum. Intensive studies leave precious little time for any extra curricular activity. At most, the students wile away whatever extra time they have in playing soccer and volleyball or just lounging around. Military training is not part of the studies as has been alleged by some outsiders but students are definitely indoctrinated to raise arms in defense of their religion.

There are 1,500 students enrolled in the school. They admit only 400 students every year out of a pool of 15,000 applicants. Almost half the slots are reserved for Afghan boys and boys from the Central Asia republics and other Muslim countries. The school offers high school education, college level studies and graduate studies. Most students end their education after high school; others go on to take college level courses in different religious subjects. A select few enter advanced studies for a doctorate.

At the graduation ceremony that is reminiscent of the medieval Islamic schools, the graduates receive their certificates and a special turban that identifies the level of their education. Prominently displayed outside the convocation hall are the framed lists of the school's former students. As mentioned above, a good number of current Taliban leaders have received their education in this school including Abdul Wakil Muttawakal, the foreign minister and Mullah Abdus Salam Zaeff, the Taliban ambassador to Pakistan. Two years ago Muttawakal presided over the graduation ceremonies and awarded the turbans.

Haqqania High School

In the summer of 1998, the Taliban were at the verge of collapse after their humiliating defeat at the hands of the Northern Alliance in the northern city of Mazar-e Sharif. When the Taliban leadership asked for help, Moulana Sami-ul-Haq closed the school and sent all able-bodied students and teachers to Afghanistan. In all 5,000 volunteers, some from other religious schools helped turn the tide in favor of the Taliban. Moulana Sami-ul-Haq carries considerable influence in Afghanistan, as I would find out during my visit to Kabul.

Over the ubiquitous cup of tea and plates of confectionery, I talked to him about a variety of subjects. The Pushtun tradition of unconditional hospitality aside, he was genuinely pleased to see me. He was comfortable that while talking to me he did not have to worry about explaining the cultural and religious nuances that can cloud the picture for the uninitiated. He mentioned how the New York Times reporter mistook the bare foot students in the classrooms as a sign of abject poverty and backwardness. The New Yorker had not realized that in Eastern cultures one always takes his shoes off before entering a room.
His answers for the most part were patent and predictable. He thought there was an international conspiracy, masterminded by the Zionists, to

thwart the Islamic revolution. He reiterated a long list of grievances against the West including their refusal to help Palestinians and Kashmiris in their struggle for independence. He was sure the tide was turning in favor of Muslims the world over. To him the Taliban were true Muslims and their interpretation of Islam was correct and legitimate. On the delicate issue of their negative attitude toward the Shia Muslims, he was willing to work with Shia religious leaders for the sake of national unity even though he considered them beyond the pale of Islam. The Moulana was sure that after the success of the Taliban in Afghanistan it was only a matter of time when a Taliban style Islamic order would be established in Pakistan. He assured me, as I would learn later, that Osama bin Laden was a Muslim hero and that Afghanistan can not make him a bargaining chip for improved relations with America.

When I told him about my intention to visit Afghanistan, he promised to facilitate my visit. The next day a packet of personal letters of introduction arrived at my residence. They were written to key figures in the Taliban government including one for Mullah Muhammad Omar, head of the state. One letter however was of particular interest. It was addressed to the rank-and-file Taliban workers in Afghanistan asking them to extend all possible courtesy and facilitate in my travels through Afghanistan. That letter alone would have been enough to open every door in Afghanistan.

In early November, 2000, I ventured into the land of the Taliban.

Jamia Dar-ul-Uloom Haqqania
Akora Khattak, District: Nowshera.
(N.W.F.P) PAKISTAN.

بسم الله الرحمن الرحيم

مجلة دار العلوم حقانيه
اکوڑه ختک ۰ ضلع نوشهره

تاریخ ۱۳ اکتوبر ۲۰۰۰

حواله نمبر

به نامه ده خداى اکرم

ګرانو او محترمو طالبانو ورونو .

السلام علیکم ور حمة الله وبرکاته ! دغه لرو څوک تاسو ته به خبر و معلومات سره ستی
عرض ده ده . چه بنابلے پروفیسر و ډاکتر محمد حسین صاحب چه دیرلرته عالم او فاضل او درزګو
سرمن کے . به امریکه کے او سیاه ته . او د طالبانو د تحریک زبردست حامی کے . او دغه ها
خلاف چه مظامنرا ده . او با مخالفانو مخربیتراخی . د ضخ دفاع هم کوی . د دوی ؤ الله
او تعاون او مرہؤ . خبرو دعاء ده مه الله تعالی دی مخ نده ته او ستاسو حامی او ناصر ؤ

والسلام

مهتم دار العلوم حقانیه
اکوڑه ختک .

---

*A letter written in Pushtu and addressed to the rank and file Taliban introduces
the author as a friend of the Taliban and requests that he may be accorded due
courtesy and extended all help during his travels through Afghanistan.*

6

The Journey Through a Devastated Land

Jalalabad - Kabul Road - Once a beautiful asphalt road has been reduced to a pothole strewn track. The Soviets used this road to move tanks and heavy machinery during the occupation of Afghanistan.

The journey through the Khyber Pass and across the frontier into Afghanistan is a journey through time. When I reached the border check post of Torkham between Pakistan and Afghanistan, a large crowd of perhaps 5,000 men, women and children had gathered on the Afghan side of the gate clamoring to enter Pakistan. They were the fresh wave of refugees fleeing the ravages of a prolonged drought and the continued fighting between the Taliban and the Northern Alliance.

It takes up to eight hours of rough driving on a pot-holed and crater-strewn road to reach Kabul, a distance of 160 miles. Along the way, the devastation is visible not only from the condition of the road but also from the abandoned villages, destroyed irrigation channels and scattered carcasses of Soviet tanks and vehicles rusting in the sandy waste land.

The famous Khyber Pass as it winds down towards Afghanistan. The distant mountains are in Afghanistan.

This was the route that every invader to India from the Persians to Alexander the Great to the Mongols took to loot the riches of India. It was also the setting for James Michner's novel, *Caravans*, about the age-old seasonal migration of nomads from the Afghan highlands to the plains of Pakistan. Rudyard Kipling captured the scene in his famous poem "The Cholera Camp":

> *When spring time flushes the desert grass,*
> *Our kafilas wind through the Khyber Pass,*
> *Lean are the camels but heavy the frails,*
> *Light are the purses but heavy the bails,*
> *When the snow bound trade of the north comes down,*
> *To the market square of Peshawar town.*

The war in Afghanistan and its aftermath has destroyed that nomadic life. On both sides of the road, the U.N. flags warn travelers of widely scattered land mines. Eleven years after their departure from Afghanistan, the ugly legacy of the former Soviet Union continues to maim and kill. Many of the mines were shaped as toys that young children found irresistible.

Welcome to Afghanistan, brother.

After having my passport stamped by the Pakistani immigration, I walked through the cast-iron gate into Afghanistan. That day on the Afghan side of the border a restive crowd of few thousand men, women and children were clamoring to get into Pakistan. They were the latest refugees fleeing a protracted drought and the ongoing war in the north of the country. A boyish looking Talib with an AK-47 assault rifle slung on his shoulder, spotted me and asked the reason for my presence in Afghanistan. Politely he directed me to a small building in the back of the bazaar to register myself.

In the small dingy room that was a combination bed room-sitting room and an office sat a bearded man in his 20s on the floor on cotton mattress. He greeted me with a wide grin and after examining my travel documents asked me to enter my name and details in a register.

Over a cup of sweetened milk tea the man asked why America was against the Taliban. He said they try hard to bend the rules to help foreigners, but the visitors always find faults with them. Recently a few Swedish women, most likely on a fact-finding mission, had gone to Afghanistan. The man said he let them through even though a *mahram* or a responsible male member of their families did not accompany them. We cannot change the word of God for the sake of foreigners who do not understand our religion.

The immigration officer had no idea about the world beyond the cast-iron gate he was guarding. Just beyond the gate in Pakistan people read the same scripture but draw a different conclusion.

As I left, he embraced me and asked me to tell Americans what real Islam is. He also advised me to hide my camera so that some of his fellow Taliban may not cause problems for me. I would receive this advise on many occasions in the coming days.

In the vicinity of villages, dirty children dressed in rags stood on the roadside with shovels in their hands. At the sight of an approaching vehicle, they would scoop a bit of dirt from the shoulder and dump it into a pothole. They would then hold their hands in front of them in the Muslim gesture of prayer and with an outstretched hand ask for a tip. They were play-acting to fix the road and pray for our safety for a monetary reward. That pathetic and sad scene was repeated time and again all the way to Kabul.

An abandoned village in the shadow of the snow clad Hindu Kush Mountains.

The Afghan daredevils:

Car travel on the once beautiful but now a rutted and pitted road to Kabul is a hair-raising experience. The drivers weave in and out of the path of oncoming traffic to dodge large potholes and big rocks that jut out of the destroyed pavement. They do that with the pedal pushed all the way to the floor.

Not weak-hearted by nature, I had to ask the driver to slow down. With a fatalistic shrug he smiled and said, "Sahiba, I will get you to your destination; either to Kabul or to your grave, whatever the Lord has willed."

It did not instill much confidence in me when I saw ample reminders of God's will on the roadside in the form of mangled vehicles. In my case, the Lord had willed for me to get to Kabul without loosing my life or limb.

The drivers on Kabul road are always in a hurry to squeeze in yet another trip in the daylight hours whether the Lord wills it or not.

Three images depicting large areas of Kabul that lay destroyed and abandoned due to the civil war that lasted from 1989 to 1994.

Kabul- A latter day Dresden

Drink wine in Kabul citadel, send round the cup again and again,
For there is both mountain and water, both city and countryside.

Emperor Babur.
In his autobiography Babur Nama

Zaheeruddin Babur the 16th-century king of Afghanistan and India
called Kabul a refreshingly
pleasant city and drew an
enchanting picture of its
beauty and its riches. He was
so smitten by the city that he
willed to be buried in Kabul.
His body was brought back
from Delhi and buried on a
hilltop overlooking the city.

Travelers and historians have always mentioned Kabul in the same
vein as Samarkand and Bukhara, the other two fabled cities of Central
Asia on the Silk Route.

Today the city is a ghost of its glorious past.
A walk through some parts of the city is like
walking through a bombed city. The ruins of
crumbling buildings twisted structures and
houses with gaping holes attest to the fierce
battles between various Mujahideen groups,
who in the process of destroying each other
ended up destroying the city. In April, 1996,

alone, 866 rockets hit the city killing hundreds of people and injuring many more. The Taliban also contributed to this devastation during their siege of the city in the summer of 1996, when they indiscriminately shelled the city with bombs and rockets. More than half the city lies in ruins and has been abandoned.

But despite the visible devastation and abject poverty, Kabul is functioning rather well. The main bazaars and markets are busy most of the time. There is plenty of wheat flour, cooking oil, and grain that comes from Pakistan. Fresh vegetables and fruits come from the countryside and are plentiful. Pakistani and Chinese imports of cloth, shoes, electric bulbs, kerosene lamps and other necessities of everyday life are easily available to those who can afford the price. The Afghan currency, never a stable commodity even in good times, has hit an all time low. A Pakistani rupee equals 1,000 Afghan rupees and buys but a single cup of tea. One American dollar is worth 50,000 Afghan rupees. Not many people

Music makers on the road to Kabul:

Two hours into our journey to Kabul, I asked the driver if he had any music cassettes. First he said he did not. Then after making sure I was genuinely interested in listening to music, he produced a worn out cassette from behind the ashtray. Ironically it was a tape of Naghma, an Afghan female singer, who now lives in Pakistan. A generation of Afghans grew up in exile listening to her haunting and nostalgic melodies about a country they knew but from a distance. Since music is banned in Afghanistan, the driver could not be caught with a cassette in his car. At every checkpoint he would discreetly hide the tape. The drivers have devised a system where they exchange music tapes with each other. On seeing an approaching taxi the driver slows down and sticks out his hand with the thumb over the palm. They slow down enough to exchange the tapes and then take off.

We drove all the way to Kabul listening to the stirring Afghan melodies while all the time risking a week in jail and having our heads shaved.

can afford even the most basic necessities.

Hunger and starvation is on the rise particularly in remote areas of the country. One recent traveler on his way from Iran to Herat, a distance of 70 miles, saw men, women and children lined up on both sides of the road begging for food.

The Taliban did not cause all the problems that the country faces. But they have significantly added to them by their medieval laws and their archaic governing structure.

Before we discuss the Taliban in some detail, let us first look at some faces and places in Afghanistan.

7

Faces and Places

The Intercontinental Hotel

The hotel sits on a hilltop overlooking the city of Kabul. The taxi driver thought the place would be suitable for a visitor from America. On that cold November evening the hotel appeared much colder than the ambient temperature. It looked cold because it was almost empty.

A young man emerged from the room behind the counter to answer my inquiry. Yes there are vacancies. Yes they have running hot and cold water. And yes they have telephone and fax facilities but no Internet. The rate was $75 for foreigners and $65 for natives.

I asked if I would qualify as a native? He eyed my shaven face, took measure of my native clothes and my fluency of Pushtu language and said, yes I would indeed. But I was in a haggling mood. 'How much off-season discount will I get,' I asked. Considering the ongoing problems of Afghanistan, the country has been off-season for 25 years. The question however baffled him. He had to go and ask the manager. He returned with an offer of $50 per day.

As he was looking for the manager, I had a chance to size up the place. The lobby was forlorn and empty, and the restaurant and coffee shop closed. The cozy little teahouse in one corner of the lobby with a samavor and carpets and cushions looked more like an exhibit in a museum than a functional teahouse in a hotel lobby.

Out of 200 rooms in the hotel only 10 were occupied. I decided I would rather stay in a flophouse in town where I would have a chance to meet common Afghans. I did not want to talk to some self-appointed foreigners on a fact-finding mission the conclusions of which had already been decided.

A mausoleum made unfit for a king

On a hill top in Kabul sits a once beautiful mausoleum that has dominated the city since 1933. It was built to honor of the reformist King Nadir Shah who was assassinated while inspecting a school. It was built with native marble brought from the eastern Nuristan Mountains. With a large basement, a spacious library and a vast landscaped courtyard it was a favorite place for the Kabulis to spend summer afternoons.

The relentless bombing of the city during the civil war took its toll on the mausoleum. The main structure has gaping holes in the domed ceiling that lets in shafts of sunlight as well as rain and snow. The walls are defaced and the courtyard littered with the marble debris. The grave and the head stone are no where to be found. Now idle boys and young men loiter in the place. I asked a young man about the building. He shrugged his shoulders and said, *"Khudai khabar, ma ta patta nishta."* (God only knows, I have no idea.) A whole generation of Afghans are growing up with no idea about their past, recent or remote.

An antique shop

The antique bazaar in Kabul is now deserted most of the time. Even during the Soviet occupation the shopkeepers had a good business. Now they wait all day for an occasional outsider, and, if they see a potential customer, they try every means to bring him into the shop.

A young shopkeeper impressed me with his smile and his easy manners. His shop, as many others, was full of Afghan handicrafts, clothes, hats, trinkets, brassware and china. Scattered among the ordinary stuff were rare antique wall hangings, Gardner china and stone lamps. When I showed no particular interest, he led me to the back of the shop. There on display were guns, musical instruments and statues. In present-day Afghanistan these items had no place in the main display area.

In the customary Afghan tradition that is as old as some the antiquities in the shop, we sat cross-legged on the carpeted floor and haggled on the price. I bought a beautiful handcrafted string instrument called rabbab and few other items. In the coming days, I would guard them carefully until my return to Peshawar.

An Afghan cafe

It was a step back in history. Except for some tables and chairs in the main section, a reluctant concession to modernity, the place was a throw back from another era.

On all floors of the split-level restaurant, guests sat on the floors that were covered with colorful handwoven carpets with a neat row of cushions along the walls. The waiters in baggy native clothes scurried around the place catering to the needs of the guests.

It was a scene reminiscent of the days of the caravans where the travelers would spend a day or two in a wayside inn called a *sarai*. In the evening they would unwind leaning against the embroidered cushions and swap stories of their travels through enchanting and exotic lands while listening to the soul-stirring Afghan music and sipping a local brew.

We sat on the carpeted floor making small talk and waiting for the cannon fire that would herald the end of the day-long fast of Ramadan. As the time approached, the waiters spread a colorful long tablecloth, a *dastarkhan*, in front of us. Soon the tablecloth was laden with piping hot dishes of Kabuli pulao, skewers of sizzling lamb meat, korma, egg plant, salad and oversized oven-hot flat bread.

After dinner, as we slid back to the comfort of the cushions along the wall, a waiter came with a towel on his shoulder, a pitcher of hot water in one hand and a brass wash basin in the other to help us wash our, by now, thoroughly greasy hands. A pot of tea and sweet condiments followed as a fitting finale to our culinary experience. But there was something sorely missing. The Taliban's ban on music has taken away the very soul of the Pushtun culture.

A Pakistani businessman

I saw him in the lobby of the hotel, a lanky tall mustachioed man
wearing shalwar-kamees, the kinds of baggy clothes that people wear
in Pakistan and Afghanistan. Except that his were of white color and
were starched, indicating that he was not a local. He was a Punjabi
businessman from Lahore and had come to Kabul to strike business
deals with the Taliban. He said Afghanistan was ripe for business
opportunities.

He wanted to build a plant to process vegetable oil, revive an abandoned bread-making factory and turn the scrap from destroyed Soviet
tanks and vehicles
into steel. He was
also there with an
offer to resurface
some of the key
highways in the
country. He invited
me to become an
investor in some of
the deals he was
going to discuss with

the government officials. He did not know a word of Pushtu or Dari,
the dominant languages of Afghanistan.

The next day he was not very hopeful about the prospects. He was
surprised that some of the key officials did not speak Urdu and English, the two languages *he* spoke. He had talked to the Taliban through

an interpreter but somehow the interpreter was not able to translate his enthusiasm into words the Taliban could understand. All they saw were dollar signs dancing in his eyes that I had also seen the night before.

In the end this writer and his money did not part.

Sears Robuck catalog and Lady Chaterley's Lover

A stroll through the bazaar of Kabul is an excursion into the past. Just down the street from my hotel, there was a row of small bookshops. They sold mostly religious books written in Afghanistan's two dominant languages, Pushtu and Dari. Some shops also sold old English books that had some how found their way to this out of the way place. There were novels, travelogues, a handyman's guide and the King James Bible. In one shop I saw a copy of *Lady Chaterley's Lover* sitting quite innocently with an old Sears Roebuck catalog. The shopkeeper was oblivious to the juicy and incendiary nature of the old English classic. He would be in big trouble if the moral police could read English.

Those old books had most likely found their way to Kabul in the company of foreign diplomats and were now at display in the bazaar. I searched for old manuscripts but found none. Most of the rare book and archaeological artifacts had found their way to the bazaars of Peshawar and to the markets of Europe.

A Roadside Photographer

It was a rare and unique sight to see an old fashion minute camera set on a tripod on the side of the road. The Taliban had banned photography in Afghanistan and had only recently allowed taking of photographs for passport and other document.

The camera, an adoption of the *camera obscura* of the 16th century, is a camera cum developing lab all contained in a small carton sized wood box was a relic from a century ago. It was in use throughout the world in the past century and up to the middle of the 19th century in the bazaars of India, Pakistan and Afghanistan. With the advent of the single reflex cameras they gradually disappeared from the scene. Somehow at the threshold of 21st century they

had made a comeback more as a cheap alternative to regular and more expensive cameras and also the ease of developing the picture on the road side as the customer waited.

The photographer, an elegant elderly Afghan, seated me on a stool in front of the camera. He took the lens cap off and exposed the plate at the pack of the darkened box for about 10 seconds. Then he disappeared under a black cover, put his hands through two sleeves and went to develop the negative. In minutes he produced three passport size grainy prints, still wet from the developing solution. He showed them for my approval, waved them back and forth to dry them and handed me the result.

Cost? 50 cents.

The shoe shine boy

He kept pestering me to let him shine my shoes. The boy, hardly eight, wore a pair of dirty old jeans, a tan coat and old tattered shoes. He carried the tools of his trade in a box strung on the shoulder by a wide strap. However, the most striking thing was his blond hair, blue eyes and fair skin. He was a living reminder of the remote and ancient history of his people. The invaders from Central Asia and Europe had not only left monuments to their presence in the area but also their genetic legacy.

I relented. While he worked on my shoes, I sat on the sidewalk and talked to him. His story was no different than those of hundreds and thousands of Afghan families who had been caught in the winds of constant turmoil in their country. He was the youngest of seven children in the family. The father had died during the civil war and now the kids were out on the street eking a meager income for the family. Many boys fall into the trap of prostitution while trying to make money for their families.

Keeper of the road barrier

To avoid the rush of slow moving traffic, we left Kabul in the wee hours of the morning for Pakistan. Twenty miles out we were stopped at a road barrier. The young Talib in charge of the crossing sat at one end of the barrier on a bench wrapped in a cotton quilt. He said the barrier would open at sunrise according to his instruction from Kabul.

He was polite but very firm.

As a last resort, I invoked his sense of Pushtun hospitality by saying that he should make an exception for a guest of Afghanistan. Somehow the tribal code of hospitality overcame his blind adherence to the orders of his superiors. He released the rope to raise the barrier but made sure ours was the only vehicle that passed on his watch.

Hayatabad Town, Peshawar.

Hayatabad is a modern township eight miles west of Peshawar City on the road to the Khyber Pass. Nestled in the foothills of the Suleman Mountains, the beautifully planned town is a study in contrasts. On the opposite side of the Khyber Road sits Nasir Bagh Afghan refugee camp, one of the oldest in Pakistan. The mud houses of the camp are stark contrast to the spacious and elegant mansions and bungalows owned by Pakistani professional drug barons and rich Afghan expatriates. Hayatabad is also the place where desperate Afghan women indulge in the world's oldest profession.

I saw a petite Afghan woman by a vegetable stand. She was dressed in rather expensive flashy clothes, an unusual sight for an unescorted woman in that part of the world. I noticed that the vendor was not very nice to the woman. When I inquired the reason for his rudeness, the man replied that the woman and many others like her are blemish on the face of humanity. All they do is to sell their bodies to well-to-do people, local as well as itinerant visitors who come here looking for women. What startled me was his remark that they all should be sent to Kabul where the Taliban would take care of them by executing them.

Peshawar has more Afghans than any city inside Afghanistan. Most of them live hand-to-mouth and survive on whatever meager help that comes from Pakistan and some Western sources. Where as the educated Afghan men do find work, how menial or poorly remunerative, educated Afghan women are not that lucky. With no man in the family to look after them, many Afghan women become sole breadwinners for their families. Some of them end up as street beggars and others are forced into prostitution.

8

The Taliban Governing Structure

The enigmatic Mullah Muhammad Omar is the head of the state but continues to live in the southern city of Kandahar. He presides over a 10-member consultative council or the Supreme Shura that is based in Kandahar. Its members include the chief justice, military chief of staff, foreign minister, interior minister, information minister and the governor of the state bank. All of them are the founding members of the Taliban movement. Two other *shuras* report to this body. One is the military shura of top commanders and the other is the Kabul Shura that essentially includes all the cabinet ministers. As is evident from the structure, many members of the two subordinate shuras also serve on the Supreme Shura.

Since the head of the state lives in Kandahar and the Supreme Shura is based in that city also, the Kandahari mullahs appear to have an upper hand in running the country. The cabinet ministers make frequent visits from Kabul to Kandahar to discuss pressing issues with the leader and get his approval.

If there is dissention within the ranks of mullahs about policy matters, it is not evident. Once a decision has been made and approved by Mullah Omar, there is no dissention or further debate. His orders are then carried out without any question. On the question of Bamiyan Buddhas, there were pragmatic mullahs who had advised against their destruction. Once Mullah Omar made the decision to destroy them, his orders were promptly carried out.

In the aftermath of the embassy bombings in August, 1998, Saudi intelligence chief Prince Turki Al-Faisal visited Mullah Omar and requested extradition of Osama bin Laden. Mullah Omar not only turned down the request he went on to verbally abuse the Saudi royal family. He could care less about the consequences, which in this case cost his regime vital financial and diplomatic support.

Qari Muhammad Farooq, Talib in charge of the strategic crossing at Pul Surkhakan where a road branches off to Lughman province.

There are approximately 35,000 rank-and-file Taliban who run the country. All jobs with some administrative or security responsibility, from high-profile government jobs to the lowly but important road check-points in the country are manned by the Taliban. A turban from any one of the hundreds of schools in Afghanistan or Pakistan is a sure ticket to a government job under the Taliban.

While outsiders have difficulty accepting or understanding the Taliban's single-minded adherence to Islam, on a personal level they are polite, truthful and self-confident with streaks of self-righteousness. I did not come across a single Talib who was discourteous, belligerent or rude. From the lowly border and check-post guards to high government functionaries they exhibited a rather high standard of personal conduct. Although, they are totally uncompromising and often belligerent when it comes to enforcing the dictates of their religion. At times, their self-righteous belligerency overshadows their more enduring qualities.

Stories are beginning to emerge where some of the Taliban have taken the law into their own hands and have executed innocent travelers for their money. In one incident in the western region of Herat, a number of Taliban stopped refugees returning from Iran, robbed them of their money, and then executed them. Independent confirmation of such incidents is difficult to obtain.

In 1998 the Taliban did carry out a massacre of 3,000 Hazara Shias and Uzbeks in the northern town of Mazar-e Sharif. Unfortunately such brutality toward the civilian population has not been limited to one side. Hazaras had done the same to the Taliban a year earlier in the same place. Somehow the brutal civil war has destroyed the age-old Afghan tradition of acceptance of diversity among its ethnic patchwork.

The Taliban rank-and-file is faithful to their education and to the system that brought them to power. They seem to be bound not by their ethnic or tribal backgrounds or political affiliations but by their common educational background. At least this is how it appears on the surface. There does not seem to be an elitist culture based on what school they attended or the level of education they attained. A turban awarded by a *madrassa* is worn with pride just as a necktie, class ring or school colors are worn in the West.

They sincerely believe that by adhering to the basic values of Islam

> **Brother, you have no beard.**
>   At another check post the guard in-
> charge peered through the window and ex-
> claimed, "Brother, you don't have a beard." I
> told him I was a *kharaji*—meaning an out-
> sider. Are you from Pakistan, he asked? When
> I said I was he went in the preaching mode
> and said, "we are all Muslims and it does not
> matter where we live. We have to follow our
> religion. Keeping a beard is part of our reli-
> gion."
>   Muslims try to imitate the deeds and
> actions of the Prophet. Keeping a beard comes
> under that category. It is not one of the tenets
> of Islam. The Taliban has elevated optional
> elements of religion to essential level.
> I thanked him for his advise and asked him to
> pray for my salvation.

they can overcome any difficulty. They are also convinced that they have been given the task and a rare opportunity for the revival of Islam. Their concept of a just Islamic society is deeply rooted in the early Muslim society of the 7th-century Arabia but without the tolerance and compassion that were hallmark of that early Islamic society. They also loath any religious innovation that strays from the traditional and often archaic interpretations.

There is a big disconnect between the way the Taliban think and the way the rest of the world, or for that matter, most Muslims think. On the question of public executions in the Kabul soccer stadium, some of the officials, including the foreign minister, said that they cannot afford to build a separate place for this purpose.

It was difficult to engage the Taliban on any discussion that was out-side the realm of religion. History, philosophy and science are not worth discussing. One subject did come under discussion rather fre-quently and that was the American policy toward Afghanistan. They were curious about, and also fascinated by America. But in the same breath they were frustrated and angry about America's lack of concern about the plight of Afghans and its refusal to recognize them as Afghanistan's legitimate rulers.

A ministry to keep the faithful in line

From a drab building in downtown Kabul, The Ministry for the Promotion of Virtues and Prevention of Vice oversees the implementation of Islamic laws in the country. It is headed by a graduate of Haqqania School in Pakistan and carries out its mission through the religious police, which is independent of other law-enforcement agencies. The ministry takes its name from a passage in the Qura'n that literally means to accept what is allowed and to reject what is prohibited. The ministry is modeled after a similar one in Saudi Arabia.

Armed with the holy license, the religious police make sure the men have proper beards, attend five daily prayers and do not listen to music. The women are ordered to stay indoors and are required to cover themselves with head-to-toe tent-like garments called *burqa* when they venture outside their homes.

A Talib from the Ministry for the Promotion of Virtues and Prevention of Vice.

The religious police wield broad powers and are the final arbiters of difference between vice and virtue. The punishments for some of the minor offences are hilarious. A man without a beard is incarcerated till he has grown one. Those caught with a music cassette spend seven days in jail and have their heads shaved. Any shopkeeper not attending prayers at the appointed hours

57

has to close his shop for a minimum of one week. Exhibiting any kind of immodesty by men lands them in jail and their heads shaved. Two years ago, the religious police arrested a visiting Pakistani soccer team and shaved their heads. They had violated the public modesty rule by playing the game in shorts. Afghanistan did apologize when Pakistan protested.

The Taliban seem to be preoccupied with beards. According to their way of thinking, they are to imitate the Prophet in his appearance, conduct and demeanor. Since Prophet Muhammad had a beard it becomes incumbent upon every adult Muslim man to have one. Somehow in their religious zeal, they do not differentiate between the obligatory and the optional. Whereas there is no room for questioning the injunctions of the Qura'n, the traditions of the prophet are considered optional. If someone wants to follow the traditions, it is considered commendable. But these traditions cannot be elevated to the level of the Qura'n, as the Taliban seems to have done.

A later day coliseum.

The Olympic Stadium near down town Kabul is a spacious place where the Kabulis used to enjoy soccer games or the ancient game of *buzz kashi* where galloping horsemen in a fierce display of horsemanship try to snatch a carcass of a sheep from the opposing team. Now the place is used for public executions and for meting out harsh punishments.

The news of an intended execution is announced in the newspaper and on the radio. In full view of the public, the person is executed by a firing squad and then hung from a crane. Stoning for adultery has been replaced by putting the accused behind a wall and then having a tank roll over the wall. Some Kabulis told me that in the beginning the Taliban also carried out chopping off the hands of habitual thieves in public.

People still talk about how the Taliban on entering Kabul stormed the U.N. compound and arrested former president Najibullah. He and a few of his advisors were summarily executed and their bodies strung in the bazaar for many days.

The beards have to be of sufficient length according to the rule. The rule states that it should be the length of one fist and two-finger breadth (in Persian *Yuk baalisht wa doo angusht*). Since that length is precisely the height of the glass chimney in a hurricane lantern, the religious police use the glass to measure the length of a questionable beard. In another bizarre practice some overzealous Taliban use metal tongs to see if the person has unshaved pubic hair. The faithful are supposed to keep their pubic hair shaved as a sign of cleanliness.

They also frown upon making any kinds of human images or taking photographs. I understood the advice of my driver and even some Taliban during my journey to Kabul not to have my camera in the open. Once arrested it takes days to sort out things and things do not move fast in Afghanistan.

The women have fared worst under the extreme Deobandi philosophy of the Taliban. Before the Taliban, women constituted one-fourth of the Kabul civil service. They staffed the entire elementary education and much of the health system. After the capture of Kabul, the Taliban, through a series of Draconian edicts, wiped the women off the public scene and pushed them behind the closed doors of their homes. They sent 70,000 girls home when they ordered the closure of

A burqa clad woman on the street in Kabul. The women are always watched by the religious police for any violation of the prescribed code of conduct.

With no schools available these young boys spend the time selling sugar cane bits on the road side.

their schools. A whole generation of Afghan boys is growing up without formal education because there are not enough male teachers to do the job and women are not allowed to teach males.

To circumvent these problems

many Afghans have sent their families to Pakistan for their children's education. But the majority of the Afghans are trapped between their desire to educate their children and a system that is willing to set aside

A woman negotiating the pavement through the cotton grill in front of her eyes.

their immediate needs for an uncertain utopian future.

A whole generation of Afghan boys (and girls) growing up without any formal education.

9

A Gentle Giant With a Medieval Mind

Meeting with the deputy foreign minister

At the Ministry of Foreign Affairs, I was received by the deputy foreign minister Abdur Rahman Zahid, a burly young man in his early 30s. He was officiating for Abdul Wakil Muttawakal, the foreign minister, who was out of the country. A large man in flowing Afghan clothes, jet-black shiny beard and the black turban of authority he filled the room with his presence but exuded a kind and gentle demeanor. Like many in the Taliban leadership he is also an "orphan" of the Afghan war. He grew up in Pakistan during the Soviet occupation and attended a *madrassa* in the southern district of Kohat.

He was apologetic that because of a delayed message from his consul general in Peshawar he was not able to receive me at my hotel. He considered it to be an honor to receive a guest of Moulana Sami-ul-Haq. We discussed a wide array of subjects, and he was refreshingly candid in his answers.

On women's education:

We are not against women's education but we do not have the facilities at this time. Once we have enough teachers, we will open schools for girls. But boys and girls must be educated separately because that is what our religion says. The old education system that the country had for 20 years was put in place by the Soviets. We need a curriculum that is consistent with our beliefs. I am sure once we overcome economic difficulties and will be able to put in place a just (educational) system.

On the absence of scientific education in Islamic schools:
We are not against scientific education. Our universities teach these courses. We start these courses after the 12th grade. Our students need to have a firm foundation in religious education before they are taught other subjects.

On the reasons why the Taliban are recognized by only three countries (a number that has been reduced to just one, Pakistan, after the start of the U.S.-led war against the Taliban):
The West does not understand our ways. The world is being dictated to by the powerful West on behalf of the Zionists. It is ironic that even though we have brought peace (to Afghanistan) by getting rid of a system of exploitation, extortion and killings, we are not recognized as the legitimate rulers of this country. By contrast they recognize (Burhanuddin) Rabbani as president of Afghanistan even though his so-called government

Ministry of Foreign Affairs.
A guard at the cast-iron gate led me to the large multi-storied handsome building where at the reception area I was greeted by Moulvi Muhammad Qasim Haleemi, director of the ministry. Mr. Haleemi, a handsome bearded man in his 40s was dressed in a nicely pressed white shalwar kameez suit and wore a black turban of authority. He greeted me warmly and said the acting foreign minister Mr. Zahid would receive me as soon as other guests left. In Afghanistan the word guest is used to designate all visitors, whether personal friends or official visitors. Despite that being the beginning of Ramadan, the Muslim month of fasting, he asked if I would like a cup of tea. He was pleased to learn that I was fasting.

The room was a beehive of activity. Visitors, natives as well as foreign aid workers dropped in to see him and Mr. Haleemi responded to their inquiries with politeness and grace that is so much part of the Afghan culture. He answered phones, and in between calls and visitors he would get on a CB radio and talk to his staff in the field about the foreign visitors expected in the city that afternoon.

controls less than 5 percent of the territory. The opposition of Western countries toward us is deeply rooted in their historic animosity toward Islam and the Muslims.

What about the role of America in helping the Mujahideen?
They did help, but they were motivated by their own strategic reasons to bleed the Soviet Union. After the war, all of them left.

On the question of foreign aid:
I do not believe that the West would give us aid even if we start doing things their way. Look, the West supported Rabbani (before the Taliban's victory) and how much aid did his government receive? Nothing! We do not think the aid should be linked to humiliating conditions. We need American assistance but cannot accept unfair conditions that America has attached for such assistance.

On harsh punishment:
Islamic punishments are just and fair because they not only punish the criminal but they also deter others. I don't understand why the criminals should have more rights than their victims. The Islamic jurisprudence is very well defined. We cannot change it.

Are there any other governments that are Islamic?
There is not a single government in the world that could be considered

> In the next room, two young aid workers were having their documents validated or extended. They appeared to be familiar with the system and knew the ropes. I talked briefly with one of them, a Frenchman, who worked for a European non-governmental aid agency in Kabul. Frustrated with the bureaucratic red tap he was in no mood to carry on a conversation. He appeared to be a bit resentful that I was being treated preferentially even though I was also a visitor like him. Familiarity with language and culture of the host country does make a difference.

as an Islamic state. Saudi Arabia, United Arab Emirates and Sudan, however, come close.

(To my surprise he did not mention their biggest benefactor Pakistan in that list)

On the Northern Alliance:
They are using 5 percent of the population as a shield for their ulterior motives. But the people living under their control are with us. The people want peace and stability that they have not been able to get under the likes of Rabbani and Ahmad Shah Massoud. They are receiving help from Iran, Russia and the U.S. but still they are unable to defeat us. They are traitors to the cause of Afghanistan.

On the conditions for compromise with the Northern Alliance:
If they stop their insurgency and accept the Islamic government (of Taliban), we will forgive them in the greater interest of our country, and they will not be punished.

On Osama bin Laden:
Osama bin Laden is our guest, and we are honor-bound to give him refuge. His services to Afghanistan during the jihad against the Soviet Union cannot be forgotten. The U.S. has linked him to some terrorist activities. We have asked the U.S. time and again to share with us the evidence against him, but they have refused. We offered to put him on trial in Afghanistan but that is not acceptable to the U.S. We even offered to hand him over to a third country for a fair trial but the U.S. has refused that offer also. We cannot hand him over to the U.S. because of mere allegations against him. Our people, and the greater Muslim nation, will not stand for it.

(According to informed sources the U.S. had shown some of the convincing evidence to Pakistan. The Pakistani interior minister General Moinuddin Haider presented the evidence to Mullah Omar in Kandahar earlier this year. The Taliban have rejected the evidence. In a recent Washington Times interview Pakistani President Pervez Musharraf said the evidence against Bin Laden is convincing.)

On the whereabouts of Bin Laden:
He is in Afghanistan. His movements are restricted because of political and security reasons. He has not run afoul of the Taliban and remains our honored guest.

Can I meet him?
It is up to our honored guest (to answer this question). As you know, we cannot put conditions on our guests. Under the present security arrangements, it would be difficult to see him. If you go to Kandahar and have audience with Amir-ul-Momineen you may bring up the subject.

On the West's attitude toward the Taliban:
The West and the U.S. have a two-face policy. On the one hand, they champion the cause of human rights, the right of self-determination and democracy, but on the other, they totally ignore the plight of Palestinians, the Kashmiris and the Chechens. You can not have two different policies on the same basic issue.

On the exclusion of women from public life:
We do not want our women to be exploited by men. When there is free mixing that is bound to happen. We have not stopped women from work. They still work in the hospitals, but they take care of only the

female patients. We will slowly integrate them in public life according to the dictates of Islam.

At the end of our interview we talked for 30 minutes. He told me about his visit to the United States a year ago. He had enjoyed meeting with the American people even though he had difficulty communicating with them in English. During the conversation, he casually asked if America would attack Afghanistan again as it had done in 1998 to retaliate the U.S. Embassy bombings in Kenya and Tanzania. I told him I had no way of knowing. It was surprising to hear a high government official in Kabul ask me about the intentions of the U.S. government.

When I asked if I could talk to the woman doctors, he invited me to visit one of the hospitals in Kabul and see for myself. But before I was allowed to go to the hospital, I had to register as a journalist with the information department.

At the information department, housed in a building next door to the ministry of foreign affairs, I was received warmly with the usual Afghan hospitality. I

The Internet connection.

I was surprised when the deputy foreign minister mentioned that Kabul was connected to the Internet and that I could check my e-mail from an office in the building.

The Internet facilities are part of the help Pakistan gives to the Taliban. Pakistan has provided 200 telephone connections to Kabul through its network in Peshawar and hence all those phones, including the one's in the government offices, have a local Peshawar number. To gain access to the Internet I dialed a local number in Peshawar. Except for sudden loss of connection that is so common in Pakistan and very annoying, the system worked well.

It was surreal to be surfing the Internet from Kabul and learning about the latest happenings in the world and in Toledo through the magic of the Internet.

filled in some forms, and they issued proper documents identifying me as a journalist. They gave me a copy of do's and don'ts but requested that I return the copy after reading for they had only one copy of the instructions. The instructions were strange. Of the dozen or so instructions I could remember the following:

1) No photography of any living object including women.
2) Photography of non-living objects such as buildings is allowed.
3) No visit to local homes allowed.
4) No photography of important government installation, airports, bridges, etc.
5) To respect the laws and traditions of the Islamic Emirate of Afghanistan.
6) Women visitors to wear proper clothes in public and cover their hair.
7) Not to report any untrue things.

10

Burqa Clad Surgeons

A clerk from the foreign affairs ministry accompanied me to Wazir Muhammad Akbar Khan Hospital located near the embassy row. It is a 250-bed acute-care hospital that caters to the needs of people within a 100-mile radius. I met the administrator of the hospital in his small office where the bearded talib was holding court on the carpeted floor. He appeared suspicious and reluctant to allow me to see the hospital. He asked me to come back the next day since it was already early afternoon and the staff was about to leave. When one of his surgeons volunteered to show me around, he relented.

Health care in Afghanistan has reached rock bottom even by the Third World standards. Infant mortality is a staggering 18 percent and a fourth of the children do not reach their fifth birthday. For every 100,000 deliveries 1,700 mothers die in the process. Life expectancy for men and women is a 44 years compared to 61 years for other underdeveloped countries. A mere third of the population has access to health care. The Taliban are not responsible for these conditions, but they have not done much to ameliorate them either.

A patient and his attendant.

69

The multistoried hospital was a chaotic mess. The old-fashioned dormitory styled wards and antiquated x-ray and rudimentary laboratory facilities were a throw-back to a past era of medicine. The wards were crowded with patients and their attendants. Some patients were on hospital beds, others on string cots brought from home and others were lying on quilts spread on the floor. The patients have to arrange for their own food, medicines and occasionally surgical supplies. The hospital staff tries hard to respond to the needs of the patients, but there are hardly any funds to provide food and medicines to patients.

Thanks to a bunch of dedicated and committed doctors, the hospital has active general surgery, urology, orthopedic and gynecology and general medicine services. With the ingenuity that is so typical of the underdeveloped countries, the Afghan physicians are able to accomplish much with the very limited resources.

In the operating rooms, I was introduced to the women surgeons that were on the staff. The Taliban's claim that women doctors are free to work is true but to a degree. The women surgeons are allowed to treat women patients only. Male surgeons work on males and also on females if there are no women specialists in the field available. The women surgeons and a few female nurses work side by side with their male colleagues but this interaction and mingling occurs only within the restricted confines of the operating rooms.

The operating rooms, like the rest of the facilities, were antiquated. A large number of patients waited outside the operating room entrance, some sitting on benches others on the cement floor, waiting for their turn. Most surgeries are performed under spinal anesthesia or general anesthesia using ether or chloroform. After surgery, patients were recovered in the ward where family and friends provide most of the post-operative care and the same for nursing care.

Surgical infection remains the biggest challenge for surgeons. In order to prevent contamination of clean operating rooms, they have set aside a few operating rooms for infected or potentially infected cases on a different floor of the hospital. Since their system of sterilization is not tight, a number of clean cases also end up with infection.

The instruments were sterilized by either boiling them in water or in a steam sterilizer. The sterilized instruments were laid on a sterile table covered with sterile towels. Throughout the day, instruments from the table were taken to the operating rooms in the periphery of the centrally located sterilization room. This system was in vogue at the turn of the century in most hospitals in the world but has been given up for more advanced but rather expensive systems. The large volume of work and lack of adequate resources have forced the surgeons to use whatever is available and do the best they can.

To meet the women surgeons, I was led to the sterilization room in my street clothes. My meeting with them took place while I stood in the doorway of the room. That was the only private place in the hospital where I could talk to them face to face. I was introduced as a Muslim surgeon from America.

Dr. Naseema Azmi is a petite, cheerful woman with a pleasant disposition and a ready smile. After graduating from Kabul University, she received training in general surgery in Kabul and is now working as a staff surgeon. The other lady surgeon, Dr. Sharifa Siddiqi, is still in training. It was the end of her shift, and she was going home. She had put on the ubiquitous light blue *burqa* over her street clothes and was about to leave. It was an odd sight to see a highly educated professional woman forced to wear a garment that to many Muslim scholars has nothing to do with religion. During our conversation, she did not cover her face, as she would on the street. A female nurse in her scrubs also joined us.

They talked about their unending workload, scarcity of resources and lack of opportunities to further their skills and education. However they were grateful to be able to practice their profession even if in a limited and secluded surroundings. Many of their sisters in other professions were not that lucky.

The surgeons and physicians receive an equivalent of $100 a month. They supplement their meager salary by seeing patients in the evenings in their homes or makeshift one-room clinics. The International Committee of the Red Cross also helps out with some financial aid.

In our hour-long talk, the subject never veered away from their work. They did not talk about their personal lives, the forced seclusion of their gender by the Taliban or their desire for a change. Even when I tried indirectly for their comments about the lack of girls' education and restrictions on their work, they were evasive. It may have been because of the presence of their male colleagues during our conversation or because they were talking to a male stranger whose outlook and affiliation they did not know. They appeared to be quite knowledgeable about their craft.

Both the male and female surgeons were extremely relaxed and polite. There was no tension during the meeting. It was ironic as well as refreshing to see some of the man-made barriers, disguised as religious dictates, set aside for the greater benefit of mankind. As a surgeon, I felt privileged to be in the company of those selfless women.

An American Relic - Ibn Sina Hospital

While driving through Kabul, I saw a familiar sight and could not resist stopping. It was Ibn Sina Hospital, and it brought back memories of my past visits to the place.

Ibn Sina Hospital

Dr. Robert Shaw, a world-renowned thoracic and cardiac surgeon from Dallas, Texas, had established the hospital in the 1960s. It was named after the 11th-century Persian-Arab physician and philosopher Avicenna. The hospital, one of its kind in Afghanistan, specialized in chest and heart surgery. In the early-1970s when I was on the faculty of Khyber Medical College in Peshawar, I made periodic visits to Kabul to learn heart surgery techniques that Dr. Shaw had pioneered in a Third World setting. Every year Dr. Shaw would take a few months off his busy academic practice in Houston to come to Kabul to teach surgical techniques to young Afghan surgeons.

The hospital was a shocking sight. It had long ceased to be what Dr. Shaw had built and developed. In his time, it was a clean, efficient and rather attractive place where young Afghan surgeons performed all types of chest surgery with excellent results. Now it was nothing more than a run down dormitory for the sick. Just like the other hospital I had visited earlier, this too was in shambles but much more so. In the open wards, patients' families and attendants cooked food on charcoal fires, nursing staff was non-existent and operating rooms closed. The only concession to modernity was a vintage x-ray machine and an old microscope in a drafty room designated as laboratory.

The staff however was much more receptive to my visit. They took me on rounds and asked my opinion on certain cases. I asked about some of the surgeons I had met there in the early-1970s. No one recognized any of the names I mentioned.

None of them knew any thing about Dr. Robert Shaw either.

The staff at Ibn Sina Hospital

11

Voices in the Bazaar

Afghanistan appears calm and tranquil but below the surface there is an undercurrent of dissent. People are reluctant to talk openly because of a vast network of informers that has always been a fact of Afghan life. Occasionally during conversation, the resentment against the Taliban comes to the surface and spills over. An open opposition to the Taliban rule has not materialized partly because the populace is still uncertain as to the validity of the Taliban version of Islam and partly because any opposition would be considered anti Islamic and therefore brutally crushed.

The population is also fearful of the drastic punishment meted out to criminals. It is the fear of harsh punishment and not their regard for a civil and just society that keeps the majority in tow. Under the Taliban law the decisions of the religious courts are final and punishments swift.

The taxi driver who brought me to Kabul was candid. While he was appreciative that the Taliban had restored law and order, he was critical

of their suppression of women and their preoccupation with beards and music. "What our religion has to do," he asked rhetorically, "with the length of facial hair or playing music?" He was quite comfortable in circumventing injunctions against music by clandestinely playing cassettes in his car.

In the Ministry of Foreign Affairs, I saw a distinguished Afghan with flowing white beard, neatly pressed native cloths, a long frock coat and astrakhan hat of lamb skin. He appeared to be well educated and well groomed and stood out in the turbaned crowd. When our eyes met, he approached me and whispered as to how lucky I was not to be living in this hellhole. Before I had a chance to respond, he walked away. He appeared to be one of the remnants of the cosmopolitan elite of Kabul.

A waiter at my hotel approached me when I was taking pictures of the Bazaar from one of the hotel balconies. He cautioned me about the prying eyes of the Taliban in the bazaar. Had he been a supporter of the Taliban, he would have asked me not to take pictures as it was prohibited by Islam. Even some of the Taliban on my way to Kabul had advised me, in the most polite way, to keep my camera hidden because some of their kind might take exceptions to a beardless Muslim from

America snapping pictures.

It is hard to imagine that the entire Afghan nation has converted to the Taliban philosophy. For sure there are voices of dissent but those voices are fearful and mute. Even in the Taliban rank-and-file there are people who realize that religious interpretation varies from time to time and from country to country. The cracks within the Taliban movement, invisible now, are bound to surface once a coherent challenge is mounted against their rule in the future. Afghan history is replete with such examples.

Throughout my stay the divide between the rulers and the ruled was very obvious. The common man on the street talked of the Taliban in the third tense *they* rather than in the first tense *we*. If their own co-religiousts Muslims feel alienated and suffocated under the Taliban, what about the religious minorities? Surprisingly, the minorities are doing rather well under the Taliban.

The Hindus of Afghanistan

Afghanistan has a long history of a vibrant and prosperous Hindu and Sikh community. They have lived in Afghanistan for generations and while keeping in touch with their spiritual roots in India, they had integrated well within the greater Afghan society. Most of them are traders and businessmen who control the cloth, currency and gold markets in all the major cities in Afghanistan. During the civil war a good number of them left the country; the majority returning to India while others made their way to the West. Still there is a thriving Hindu and Sikh community in Kabul.

The photography shop of Ram Parkash has been a familiar sight in

Kabul for more than 100 years. It sells cameras and photographic equipment and, before the Taliban ban on photography, offered sittings for formal photographs. With the photography declared as an un-Islamic pastime, there is hardly any demand for their services now. In recent months however the regime has relaxed the ban and has allowed photographers to make passport photos, men only, for travel documents. A third generation Parkash by the name of Ram Saran runs the business.

A visit to Ram Saran's shop is a retro visit to a photography shop of the 1960s and 1970s. The merchandise is old and outdated; early versions of Nikon, Kodak Retina and Rolly Flex cameras and lenses displayed in glass showcases and wall cupboards. A few old posters of natural scenes add some photographic perspective to the shop. Unlike photography shops outside Afghanistan, no images of any living object, men or beast, are displayed in the shop.

In his Afghan clothes and saucer shaped round woolen cap, Ram Saran could pass for any Afghan on the street. He speaks fluent Persian, Pushtu, Urdu and Punjabi; the last language a concession to his Indian roots. Before the Taliban, Ram Saran and his family had suffered at the hands of the warring Mujahideen. They had been, as others, the victims of kidnappings for ransom and subject to frequent extortions. Now they lived in relative peace. On the question of the freedom to practice his religion, he said they have full freedom to practice their religion. Then why does he sport a beard, I asked? To him it was much more comfortable to conform even though as a Hindu he had the right not to sport one. Before the Afghan war, their children attended regular schools and received religious education either at home or at the temple. With the Afghan education system in ruins, they now teach their children at home.

Though their numbers had dwindled in Kabul in recent years, there were still a couple hundred Hindu families in Kabul. The relentless shelling between the warring Mujahideen during the civil war destroyed a number of temples but there were still a dozen or so functioning in the city.

The Taliban made news early this year for requiring Hindus to wear yellow patched that would distinguish them from Muslims. While this edict reminded the world of the Nazi era practice of requiring Jews to wear distinctive labels and tattoos, this action of the Taliban was rather innocent. The Hindus were asked to wear distinctive yellow patches to prevent their harassment at the hands of the religious police who are in the habit of pushing everyone on the street into a mosque at prayer time.

A shrine to celebrate Sikh Gurus

While an Afghan Hindu might be able to melt effortlessly in the monolithic Afghan landscape, Sikhs stand out because of their colorful turbans, beard nets and steel bracelets. I ran into Kanwal Singh, a dignified elderly Sikh gentleman in a subterranean market one afternoon.

Sikhs are wonderfully joyous people with an abiding sense of humor and an adoring simplicity. Singh's family, like Ram Saran's, had lived in Kabul for many generations. He considered himself an Afghan but was unabashed about his religion and his customs. He directed me to a Sikh *Gurdwara* (the Sikh place of worship) in another part of the city. Located in the warehouse section of the city, the gurdwara had the look and feel of a functional place of worship. Painted murals of Sikh history adorn its walls and the framed paintings of their spiritual leaders, the Gurus, hang in different rooms. A large room is used as prayer area for the ritual reading of Garanth Sahib, the Sikh holy book. A part of the complex, as is the tradition among the Sikhs, is used as a guesthouse for the traveling Sikh families.

The main gate to the gurdwara was open, and there was no evidence that the place was under siege or that entry was restricted. Like Ram Saran, the Hindu photographer, Inder Jeet Singh, the keeper of the place, was very comfortable with the Taliban. He said they hold regular services on the premise for about 100 Sikh families who still live in Kabul. A large number of them, just as Hindus, had left the country. Many Afghan Sikhs now live in Peshawar among the Afghan refugees.

12

The Taliban and Their Honored Guest Osama bin Laden

The story of Arab-Afghans in Afghanistan

As mentioned a great number of Muslim youth responded to the call of holy war in Afghanistan in the early-1980s and flocked to Pakistani border town of Peshawar for deployment against the Soviet forces. They came from all parts of the Muslim world as well as from America and Europe. To them the war against the Soviet Union was an unambiguous and clear-cut struggle between good and evil. Though the majority of them came from Arab countries, the label Arab-Afghans was used for all foreign mercenaries except those from India and Pakistan. At the height of the Afghan War there were 35,000 young men fighting on the side of the Mujahideen. The majority of them had come from the Middle East.

In Afghanistan they found an outlet for their yearning to redeem their religion and their honor that has been, according to them, so mercilessly trampled by outsiders. This was their chance to fight against an infidel army and help establish a just Islamic order. To many this was an answer to their personal frustration and disappointment they had felt in their home countries at the hands of pro-Western governments. Osama bin Laden was one such young man.

Osama bin Laden was born in Saudi Arabia in 1957. His father was from Yemen and his mother a Saudi citizen. Under the patronage of Saudi royal family his father's construction business flourished. Osama bin Laden and his 56 siblings inherited their father's enormous fortune.

Bin Laden studied business in King Abd al-Aziz University in Jeddah but changed to Islamic studies and after graduation worked for the family business. As many other young Arabs, Osama was also affected by the Soviet invasion of Afghanistan and attracted to the struggle against the Soviet invaders. Between 1980 and 1982 he made frequent trips to Peshawar but his contribution was limited to financial support of the Mujahideen. In between his visits to Peshawar, he raised funds from Saudi donors for the war effort.

In 1982 he settled down in Peshawar and opened camps for the training of Arab youths. In these camps, scattered all along the long Afghan-Pakistan border, the Central Intelligence Agency trained these young men who would later be called Arab-Afghan. Using Saudi money and American arms the Arab-Afghans were trained in guerilla warfare. At the time, according to his own account, he was helping out with the war effort as representative of Saudi Arabia. In time, he set up camps inside Afghanistan in area controlled by the Mujahideen. In all these camps, the volunteers received not only training in warfare but also a hefty dose of Wahhabi Islam. It was this uncompromising extreme Wahhabi Islam that alienated many non-Pushtun Afghans and some Pushtun Afghans as well.

After the defeat of Soviet Union, Bin Laden set up Al-Qaeda, as a welfare organization for Arab Afghans and their families. As Afghanistan sank into civil war, Bin Laden left Afghanistan and went back to Saudi Arabia but continued his welfare work for Arab-Afghan families, many of whom had now settled in Saudi Arabia.

If Osama bin Laden had harbored resentment toward the West, it was not evident during the Afghan war. This came to the front only after the Iraqi invasion of Kuwait. He was incensed by the posture of his country of Saudi Arabia during that conflict. His offer to raise an army of the veterans of Afghanistan war in support of Saudi Arabia was spurned by the Saudi royal family. For Osama bin Laden, it was the duty of Muslims to defend the Saudi holy land against the expansionist designs of Saddam Hussain. When King Fahad invited American

In their seven year rule, the Taliban while seeking recognition by America, steadfastly refused to make Osama bin Laden a bargaining chip. The cartoon was published in the Frontier Post in 1998 and is reproduced with the permission of the cartoonist Muhammad Zahoor.

troops to the kingdom, the die was cast. Bin Laden lost his faith in the House of Saudi and from that point on he would consider his own country a traitor to the cause of Islam. His vociferous opposition to American forces on Saudi soil led the Saudi government to declare him *persona non grata* and in due course it stripped him of his Saudi citizenship. In 1992 he left Saudi Arabia for Sudan.

At the time Sudan was undergoing an Islamic revival under the leadership of charismatic and scholarly Hassan Turabi. While in Sudan, Bin Laden started many welfare projects in the country and also helped open and fund terrorist training camps in Sudan, Egypt, Somalia and Yemen. And he continued to instigate Muslims to oppose American interests in the world and to rise against the Saudi royal family for allowing the continued presence of American forces on the sacred Saudi soil. Within two years, he outgrew his welcome and, under American and Saudi pressure, Sudan asked him to leave. According to Prince Turki Al-Faisal, the minister in charge of security in Saudi Arabia, Sudan was willing to send Bin Laden back to Saudi Arabia but wanted guarantees that he would not be tried in a court of law. Saudi Arabia refused the deal.

Now Afghanistan was the only place where Bin Laden was welcome. So in May, 1996, he moved back to Afghanistan. He continued to direct his Al-Qaeda worldwide network from his headquarters in the southern city of Kandahar. With his presence in Afghanistan, Al-Qaeda terrorist camps took on a new dimension and importance. Afghanistan became the meeting point for terrorists who not only shared a common faith but also shared the hatred of a common enemy America. A financial and terrorist network with global reach would coordinate attacks against the common enemy.

An elite group of well-educated and highly motivated young men within the Al-Qaeda network helped these efforts. These ultra funda- mentalists belong to Takfir wal Hijra, a sub group within Al-Qaeda. The "Takfiris" as the followers of this extreme group are called, came to surface in the mid-1990s when a number of them were killed during a shootout with the police in the Pakistani border town of Peshawar. Their philosophy allows them to set aside even the most sacred tenets of their religion in the interest of accomplishing their mission. They practice the old tradition of Taqayya, holy fraud or deviousness that allows them to hide their true faith from their enemies while living among them and even adopt the ways of their enemies to avoid suspi- cion.

Osama bin Laden was a good fit for the Taliban. With his help the Taliban could articulate their own vision of Islam and the enemies of Islam and try to influence the opinions in the Muslim world to their way of thinking. Their cozy relationship was further strengthened when bin Laden befriended Mullah Muhammad Omar, the supreme leader of Afghanistan.

Bin Laden's first pronouncement of war against America and Saudi Arabia was issued soon after his return to Afghanistan when he de- clared that "the walls of oppression and humiliation can not be demol- ished except in a rain of bullets." There were many more to follow. In 1998 Al-Qaeda issued a religious edict, a *fatwa*, that in no unclear terms outlined its intentions: "The ruling to kill the Americans and their allies, civilians and military, is an individual duty for every Muslim who can do it in any country in which it is possible to." The bombings of U.S. embassies in Kenya and Tanzania soon followed. In another pronouncement his Al- Qaeda Organization warned of a rain of aircraft from the skies and warned Muslims in the West not to live or work in tall buildings.

Osama bin Laden has been on the CIA radar screen for a long time. As his role in supporting terrorism against the United States became more evident, a decision was made at the highest levels of the U.S. government to either capture him or to eliminate him. Many attempts were made with the help of Afghan informers and the Inter Services Intelligence Agency of Pakistan, but each time he eluded his pursuers. As the covert search intensified he retreated into the mountain hideouts around Kandahar.

Why do the Taliban protect bin Laden at any cost? Would there be a time when the Taliban in the greater interests of their nation hand him over to his pursuers? The answer to this intriguing question is rather simple. In a tradition that is as old as their people, tribal protection is a *sine qua non* for survival amid hostile and often warring tribes. Pushtun hospitality and the tribal code demand that a guest once accorded protection may not be abandoned even if the guest turns out to be an enemy. This mind set was evident when Mullah Omar in an interview with Rahimullah Yusafzai, a respected Pakistani journalist, defended Afghanistan's protection of bin Laden. He said that in his lifetime half of Afghanistan has already been destroyed. He was ready to see the other half destroyed rather than give up Osama bin Laden.

As of now, the Taliban are fiercely defending and protecting Osama bin Laden, whom they call an honored guest.

13

Conclusion

The instability triggered by the abolition of monarchy in 1973 and the subsequent Soviet occupation in 1979 continues to haunt the soul of Afghanistan. The Taliban are the latest arrivals on the scene who have dealt a severe blow to the delicate ethnic balance and tribal structure of Afghan society. They have done it in the name of Islam, but their Islam is alien to most Muslims in the world and even to a great number of Afghans themselves.

Afghanistan is also an arena where the United States, Russia, India, Iran, Saudi Arabia and Pakistan are vying for dominance and trying to influence the balance through their proxies. Pakistan and Saudi Arabia were on the side of the Taliban. With the official Saudi indifference toward the Taliban, Pakistan is the only country on their side now. That in turn has isolated Pakistan from the world. The Taliban, on the other hand, have also snubbed Pakistan on the question of Osama bin Laden, the Buddha statues and the treatment of their Muslim minorities and continue to influence Pakistani politics through Pakistani religious parties and their *madrassas*. Now Pakistan's very existence is at stake due to forces unleashed within its borders.

A pervasive gun and drug culture, radical fundamentalism and an unending spiral of sectarian violence are destroying the basic fabric of Pakistani society. There is wide spread sympathy for the Taliban among not only the Pakistani religious parties but also in the uneducated and marginally educated masses. Buoyed by success of the

Taliban in enforcing an Islamic order, the Pakistani religious parties are working toward bringing a similar change in Pakistan as well. Traditionally, the Pakistani religious parties have had a dismal record at the polls, but they have a great nuisance value in organizing violent street demonstration.

Another, more immediate concern is the pro-Taliban leaning of some of the top brass in Pakistani army. The powerful Inter Services Intelligence Agency of the Pakistan army has a long history of interfering in Pakistani politics and has been the force behind the success of the Taliban.

Despite all this Pakistan has remained a staunch supporter of the Taliban. In a clear violation of the American-inspired U.N. embargo, it supplies them with food, fuel and ammunition. It also continues to care for the 2 million Afghan refugees that live within its borders. In part, Pakistan's support is because of its own Pushtun population who would not tolerate the suffering of their tribal kin.

To the north of Afghanistan the Central Asian republics of Turkmenistan, Uzbekistan, Tajikistan, Kirgizstan and Kazakhstan are concerned about the export of the Taliban style fundamentalism to their countries. the same fears haunt Russia and India because of their own problems with the independence movements in Chechnya and Kashmir. They all blame the Taliban for fomenting dissension by supporting local insurrections in their countries. Pakistan gets blamed as well for its support of the Taliban. This has placed Pakistan in an unenviable isolated position in the world.

And then there is what the veteran Pakistani journalist Ahmed Rashid

> **Torkham border crossing.**
> There is a couple hundred yards of no man's land that separates Torkham border crossing between Afghanistan and Pakistan. One has to walk that strip to enter either country.
> As I walked toward the Pakistani border I was struck by the music wafting over the area from a teahouse beyond the checkpoint. I had not realized how comforting the sound of music could be after having spent time in music-less Afghanistan. An overwhelming sense of freedom came over me.
> At the teahouse, I ordered a pot of milk tea and sat outside the teahouse in the warm November sunshine sipping the precious brew. As I listened to the stirring Pushtu music, I realized that by banning music in Afghanistan, the Taliban had taken away the very soul of the Pushtun culture.
> While sitting on the string cot, drinking my cup, I heard Ahmad Khan's voice singing the poetry of the 17th-century Pushtun poet Rahman Baba:
>> *Many people I remember*
>> *Tasting power in my day*
>> *And I saw them fade away*
>> *Into dust and ember.*
>> *Sandal-trees would chafe and shiver,*
>> *Following the ancient law,*
>> *Box-tree branches for the saw,*
>> *Fell with silent quiver.*
>> *On the site of solemn graveyards,*
>> *Mighty structures rested once,*
>> *Now they are in dust ensconced,*
>> *Destiny is wayward.*
> How true indeed.

calls the New Great Game. Turkmenistan's large oil and gas reserves need a short route through Afghanistan and Pakistan to reach the Arabian Sea. The pipeline project has been resurrected many times and then abandoned because of the ongoing war in the north of Afghanistan that precludes heavy investment in the project. Since 1992 when Turkmenistan became independent, international oil politics and conflicting regional interests have also muddied the waters in Afghanistan. A stable Afghanistan is not in the interest of some of its neighbors who would benefit from a pipeline going through *their* territories rather than through Afghanistan. But an unstable Afghanistan with a gloabal terrorist reach is not in the best interest of anyone.

In the shifting sands of Afghan politics, a government based solely on outdated religious interpretations will not be able to withstand the strong surge of ethnic sensitivities and tribal loyalties. In a conflict between tribal traditions and religious practices the religion almost always ends up on the back seat. The long and tortured history of Afghanistan attests to that fact.

Epilogue

When I finished writing the manuscript of this book in August, 2001, the Taliban were in full control of Afghanistan. The Northern Alliance, a contentious group of ethnic factions, was not only fighting their common enemy, the Taliban, but each other as well. The Afghan government headed by Burhanuddin Rabbani, temporarily based in the northern Afghan town of Faisabad, was in disarray. Claiming to represent Afghanistan and recognized by the world community, the government controlled less than 10% of the country and the people in areas under its control did not fare any better than those controlled by the Taliban.

But that was before the fateful September 11, 2001.

The terrorist attacks on the World Trade Center in New York, the Pentagon in Washington DC, and downing of a commercial airliner in Pennsylvania brought in sharp focus the Taliban-Osama bin Laden connection and led to a declaration of war on the Taliban, their 'honored ' guest Osama bin Laden, and his world-wide Al-Qaeda terrorist organization. Five weeks of relentless bombing by the US and Britain has weakened the Taliban's hold on the country but has not totally crushed them. Kabul and most of the northern and western cities have fallen to the Northern Alliance. Kunduz in the north and Kandahar in the south are the only remaining cities still under the Taliban control. In due course they will also fall.

The power struggle between Afghanistan's patchwork ethnic groups has begun in earnest. If past history, remote as well recent, is any guide in predicting the future of the country, it does not look promising.

The meteoric rise of the Taliban was in part due to their noble intentions of getting the country rid of corrupt Mujahideen leaders, drug barons and petty warlords. They were true to their promise to bring law and order to a mostly lawless country. However in the bargain they also imposed a harsh and inhumane religious system that was an aberration of the true face of Islam. In a 'what if' exercise it is interesting to speculate as to what would happened to Afghanistan if Osama bin Laden would have gone to Saudi Arabia instead of landing in Afghanistan in 1994. The Afghan women would still be living a miserable existence under the burqas, girls would still be deprived of education and the country would still be ruled by a bunch of bearded zealots in the name of Islam. The West would have brushed off the Taliban as a minor irritant on the conscience of the world.

But Bin Laden *did* come to Afghanistan, breathed new life in the Al-Qaeda organization and in turn changed the course of world. Afghanistan is back on center stage.

A mad rush in now under way to install a representative government in Afghanistan. Various ethnic factions are vying for a dominance in such a setup. This was evident by the hasty entry in Kabul of the forces of Northern Alliance on November 14, 2001, even though they were expressly told by the US not to do so. Kabul has given them the advantage of ground realities as well as an opportunity to settle some old scores. In Kabul the victors were not as indiscriminate in killing the Taliban soldiers and foreign mercenaries as they had done in Mazar-e-Sharif a week earlier.

Of all the countries in the region, Pakistan has the highest stakes in the make up of the next Afghan government. The Northern Alliance, composed of Tajik, Hazara and Uzbek factions, is clearly hostile to Pakistan for its support of the Taliban. For a brief period, after the events of September 11, 2001, there was a common rallying point between the Alliance and Pakistan. They both supported a role by the exile king Muhammad Zahir Shah in a new government. So did the United States of America. Since occupying Kabul the Alliance has now back peddled on their initial intentions. The figure head president of the Northern Alliance government, Burhanuddin Rabbani, would welcome the king back to Afghanistan but only as an ordinary citizen and rules out any public role for him. Iran, sensitive to its own monarchal past, is also opposed to the return of the former king to Afghanistan.

At this time in late November 2001, Afghanistan has effectively reverted back to pre-Taliban era. In the north the notorious Uzbek general Abdur Rashid Dostum has regained control of Mazar-e-Sharif. He is known for changing sides to suit his own interests. His defection from the ranks of the last communist government of Afghanistan helped topple Najibullah and paved the way for the Mujahideen to come to power. Like a chameleon he has changed his colors from a diehard communist to a nationalist to an Islamist. In the western city of Herat the previous Tajik chieftain Ismail Khan has returned from exile in Iran and has taken control of that city. In Kabul the Tajik leader Burhanuddin Rabbani and his Defense Minister General Muhammad Fahim, also a Tajik, have staked their claim to the capital.

In the Pushtun areas the situation is not very clear at the moment. Two previous governors of Pushtun provinces are vying for control of their former provinces. In the eastern Pushtun city of Jalalabad, Younis Khalis is back and has warned the Northern Alliance to stay out of his province. In the southern province of Kandahar the Taliban are still in control but a former governor Gul Agha Sherzai is waiting in the wings for the Taliban to fall. Two other Pushtun leaders, Pir Syed Ahmad Gilani favored by Pakistan and Hamid Karzai supported by the US, are also waiting for the end of the Taliban to claim a leadership role in a post-Taliban government. One other promising Pushtun leader Abdul Haq was caught by the Taliban while drumming up support in the Pushtun tribal hinterland and was promptly executed.

Individual fiefdoms and personal strongholds are not the answer to Afghanistan's future. In order to unify the country under a coherent central government a broad-based government has to be formed in a relatively short time. The political vacuum created by the hasty departure of the Taliban from Kabul needs to be filled by a representative government. On that count the Northern Alliance's government of Burhanuddin Rabbani falls short. It does not have representation from the dominant Pushtun tribes and thus is not acceptable to the US and the UN. Under pressure from their benefactor the US, they have finally agreed to take part in a conference scheduled in Bonn on November 27, 2001. All factions of the Afghan ethnic patchwork are expected to attend the conference in proportional representation. It will not be an easy process considering their past performances.

Afghanistan's neighbors are also anxious to have a stable and friendly government in Kabul. Iran's concerns are mostly for the welfare of Shia Hazara tribe in the northwest of the country. The Taliban were particularly brutal to Hazaras whom they consider heretics and outside the pail of Islam. China has had troubles within its heavily Muslim

Zinjiang Uygur Autonomous Region where the Taliban had fueled a small indigenous independent movement. The Central Asian Republics of Tajikistan, Uzbekistan and Turkmenistan had also been fearful of religious extremism coming into their countries from across the border. A friendly and peaceful Afghanistan is necessary for re-opening of the ancient trade routes between the Indian subcontinent and Central Asia. And a peaceful Afghanistan is also necessary for the construction of a pipeline from Turkmenistan to Pakistan and India through Afghanistan.

As mentioned earlier Pakistan has the biggest stake in the make up of the future government of Afghanistan. After the creation of Pakistan in 1947, an unfriendly Afghanistan carried out a vicious international campaign for the return of border areas it had ceded to British India in 1893. Pakistan, ever sensitive to its own Pushtun population of 15 million, ignored the belligerency of its western neighbor and kept the supply routes to Afghanistan open. Then, as now, Pakistan remains the vital lifeline for the land locked Afghanistan.

A friendly Afghanistan is also necessary for Pakistan to have strategic depth on its western frontier in order to pay full attention to its eastern front with India. Pakistan and India share a long border and have gone to war three times over the Himalayan state of Kashmir since their independence 54 years ago.

A stable Afghanistan is also necessary for the return of three million refugees who have lived in Pakistan since the Afghan war. The refugees' continued presence in Pakistan has caused trouble for successive Pakistani governments since 1990. The bulk of refugees are Pushtuns and an estimated 15% are now fully integrated within the Pushtun population of Pakistan. With time greater numbers will end up staying in Pakistan for good. It will be difficult for Pakistan to seek their return to Afghanistan under a government dominated by the Northern Alliance.

After the Taliban are gone, Pakistan will also have to deal with the pro-Taliban movements within its borders. When Pakistan was the main supporter of the Taliban, Pakistani religious parties vigorously promoted a similar ideology in Pakistan in the hope of bringing a similar Taliban style government in their country. Now that Pakistan, by switching sides, has hastened the fall of the Taliban, the Pakistani religious parties are still actively promoting Taliban style resurgence in Pakistan. Heeding the call of *jihad* against the infidel USA and Great Britain, their leaders whipped up public emotions and sent thousands of poorly trained and poorly equipped volunteers into Afghanistan. Many of them were killed in action and many more were executed by the Northern Alliance when they captured the northern city of Mazar-e-Sharif on November 11, 2001. Many more face a similar fate when the northern city of Kunduz falls. The same is to be expected after the fall of Kandahar in the south.

There are thousands of Pakistani and Arab-Afghans fighting on the side of the Taliban. These Arab-Afghans are mostly from the Middle East but some are from Chechnya. They are more committed to the cause of Islam than many of the Taliban. They have fought with unmatched determination and ferocity and have in many instances chosen death over surrender. They have also at times killed Taliban soldiers when those soldiers wanted to defect to the other side. Imbued with the spirit of their just cause they are totally ignorant of the tribal make up of the Afghan society. In Afghanistan loyalties are always conditional and are subject to changing circumstances.

Northern Alliance has captured thousands of foreign mercenaries during its sweep of the north. Many more are likely to be captured as the Taliban flee their remaining stronghold in the south. While the Northern Alliance has shown some mercy towards the Taliban soldiers, they have been brutal to the foreigners. The selective massacre of Pakistanis and Arab-Afghans in Mazar-e-Sharif and to a lesser degree in Kabul underscores their attitude towards the foreign soldiers on their soil. What would they do with the captured foreigners? The United States is vehemently opposed to repatriating captured Pakistani, Arab and Chechen soldiers to their home countries for the fear that they would create havoc in their own home countries and would be a constant threat to America and the West. In so many words the American secretary of defense Donald Rumsfeld has hinted that he would not mind the elimination of those mercenaries.

A period of uncertainty lays ahead for Pakistan. At this juncture however Pakistan has an unprecedented opportunity to curb the rising tide of militant fundamentalism and stop the process of Talibization within its borders. The military government of Pervez Musharraf has been timid in dealing with the religious parties in the past. Under threat of massive street protests, it backed off from plans to take over *madrassas* and to disarm the population. With the main rallying point, the Taliban, out of the way and with the infusion of badly needed economic aid, Pakistan should be able to contain militant religious parties.

Afghanistan can not be put on a firm political and economic footing by throwing money at it. It will require the physical presence of outside forces possibly under the aegis of the UN and containing troops from Muslim countries. Already a proposal to send Indonesian, Bangladeshi and possibly Jordanian forces under Turkish command has gained support in the UN. These forces could help restore law and order and shore up the provisional government in Kabul. But at the end of the day they will have to leave and let Afghans run their own show. Would the Afghans continue on the path to democracy and economic revival or would revert back to the old ways is question that is very difficult to answer.

Herein lies the biggest challenge for the international community in general and the United States in particular. While a failure in Afghanistan would have disastrous long-term consequences, a formula for sure success also remains illusive. In the quick sands of Afghan ethnic politics, loyalties change more frequently than the notoriously unpredictable weather in the Hindu Kush Mountains. An ongoing presence of foreign troops in Afghanistan would be surely be exploited by ethnic rivals and prove the old saying that Afghanistan has always proven to be a graveyard for those who dared to stay too long even if they had come not to fight but to help.

The rise of the Taliban phenomenon was a major upheaval in the long and tortured history of Afghanistan. The events leading to the fall of Taliban were of their own making. When a desperately poor country armed with nothing more than misplaced religious fervor takes on a superpower, results can be predictably disastrous.

But unlike the victors of the past, the US has committed to rebuild the country and its institutions. Perhaps there is hope for a new Afghanistan emerging from the rubble of a destroyed land. But in the end the Afghans themselves have to overcome their own tribal and ethnic inconsistencies to make it work. They failed miserably in governing themselves after the defeat of the Soviet Union. If they were not able to rule the country in the after glow of a spectacular victory over a super power, how would they make it happen now? Or to be more realistic, *can* they make it happen?

Only time will tell.

November 27, 2001

Bibliography

Ahmed, Akbar S., Living Islam, BBC Books, London, England 1993

Ahmed, Akbar S., Islam Today, A Short Instruction to the Muslim World. IB Tauris Publishers, London NY 1999

Dupree, Louis, Afghanistan, Princeton University Press, 1980

Dupree, Nancy Hatch, A Historical Guide to Kabul, Afghan Tourist Organization, Kabul, 1970

Hussain, S. Amjad, Peshawar, A Short History, Interlit Foundation, Peshawar, 2000

Metcalf, Barbara, Islamic Revival in British India 1860-1900, Royal Book Company, Islamabad 1982

Rashid, Ahmed, Taliban, Yale University, New Haven 2000

Roy, Oliver, Afghanistan, From the Holy War to Civil War, Princeton University,1995

Appendix A:

Afghanistan at a Glance

Size: 251,739 sq. miles
Terrain: Mostly rugged mountains; plains in the north and Southwest.
Population: 26 million (2001 estimate)
Capital: Kabul 2.5 million
Life expectancy: 46.2 years
Percapita GDP: $800

Ethnic makeup: Pushtun   38%
                   Tajik   25%
                   Hazara   19%
                   Uzbek   6%
                   Other   12%

Languages: Dari (Afghan Persian) and Pushtu are official languages spoken by 43% and 42% of the population respectively. Eleven percent speak Turkik languages and remaining 4% speak about 30 minor languages.

Religion: Sunni Islam   84%
                   Shia Islam   15%
                   Other (Hindu, Sikhs) 1%

Appendix B:

Reprinted Articles

The Guns of Darra

Toledo Magazine, March 29, 1981

When Spring Time Hushes the desert grass,
Our Kafilas wind through the Khyber pass,
Lean are the camels but heavy the frails,
Light are the parses hut heavy the bales,
When the snowbound trade of the north comes down,
To the market square of Peshawar town.

—Rudyard Kipling, The Cholera Camp

Twenty miles south of the Pakistani frontier town of Peshawar, on a narrow asphalt road not too far from the Khyber Pass, one finds oneself in a roadside bazaar which appears all of a sudden out of nowhere. The bazaar and the surrounding hamlets are called Darra Adam Khel, or the Adam Khel Pass. The pass in its southward journey winds through the barren mountains—inhabited by the Afridi tribes of the northwest frontier of Pakistan—to the cantonment of Kohat.

This tiny place is playing an important role in the war between Afghanistan's Mujahideen (freedom fighters) and the Russians, as it has in the past century between its own tribes and the British.

On entering the bazaar, one is struck by the echoes of scattered gunfire, and by the display of small arms and ammunition in the shops. Peering into the shops, one gets the feeling of looking into a candy store, except that the merchandise is not candy but guns—pistols and revolvers hung on bare walls, as well as various types of ammunition displayed in neatly arranged glass cases.

The Sun industry of Darra grew out of necessity in the latter part of the last century. The Pathan tribesmen of Darra have never been subdued by any of the countless invaders who came down from central Asia to the plains of India through the mountains of the Hindu Kush. In the last century it was the British who, after subduing the rest of the Indian sub-continent, were trying to get a foothold in the area west of the Indus River.

Lacking the sophistication of these latest intruders, the Pathans fought the British with their bows and arrows and swords and daggers. Guns stolen from the British cantonments served as prototypes for these ingenious tribesmen, who in a short time perfected the art of gunmaking.

Thus a cottage industry sprang up in these mountains where the tribal people, using ordinary tools, crafted exact replicas of the famous British guns—the long, brass-bound, muzzle-loading "Jezail," the Martini-Henry, and later the Lee Enfield .30 3. They used these arms to raid with impunity the British barracks all along the ill-defined frontier. Although the foothills of the Hindu Kush no longer echo with the galloping British cavalry, the craft of gunmaking still flourishes.

Until the Russian invasion of Afghanistan, Darra supplied local tribes with light ammunition. For in a feudal tribal society the boys are taught early to handle a gun, and every man carries a gun as part of his dress and as a symbol of his manhood. A Pathan's attachment to his gun is exceeded only by his love for his son and his land. However, the Soviet invasion has brought new demand to the industry.

Lacking a regular source of guns and ammunition, the freedom fighters, many of whom belong to these tribes, have relied more and more on the craftsmen of Darra. Occasionally a captured Russian bazooka is brought to the bazaar and sold to an eager craftsman. Within a few days, copies of the gun are made and sold to freedom fighters. These guns are carted on camels and horses over the rugged mountains to the heartland of Afghanistan.

Occasionally one comes across small cannons hidden in the mud-walled dwellings surrounding the bazaar. These cannons, which also are locally made, find their way to Afghanistan and are used to fight the Soviet occupying forces.

Most of the guns are still made by hand. At places, gasoline or diesel motors are used to run a maze of belts performing different chores, but the common sight is still that of a young boy using a hand-driven drill to make the gun barrels. A locally made Lee Enfield rifle can be purchased for $300 to $400 and a round of ammunition for 20 cents.

Since the Soviet occupation of Afghanistan, millions of Afghans—rich and poor—have fled their native land. Although Pakistan is not the only country that borders Afghanistan (the Soviet Union and Iran also have common borders), most of the exodus has been to the frontier areas of Pakistan.

In the age-old tradition of the Afghan nomads who descend to the plains of Pakistan in winter and return to the Afghanistan highlands in summer, these refugees also have taken this historic path to escape the Soviet occupation. It is not only the tribal affinity between the people living on both sides of the border that binds Afghans and Pakistanis together, but also a common language and religion.

Refugees have settled in tent cities on the vast plains around Peshawar. Over the last one and a half years, they have built modest dwellings of mud and brick around these tents. Driving on the Grand Trunk Road on the way to Peshawar, one is struck by the mile-long rows of tents and makeshift dwellings. The wealthier Afghans have bought or rented property in Peshawar itself.

The strain on the local economy has been severe. In the best of times it is difficult to imagine how a half million people could live off the available resources, which until now were barely enough for the 250,000 local inhabitants.

Many of the Afghan men go to the heartland of Afghanistan to fight for months on end and then return to Peshawar to get new supplies. All the freedom fighter organizations are headquartered in Peshawar. Although some arms have reportedly been supplied by China and Egypt, there still is no steady supply of military hardware to these people.

Because of its own vulnerability, Pakistan does not overtly supply the military hardware to the Mujahideen. At best, Pakistan has an uneasy accommodation with the freedom fighters. Mujahideen continue to co-ordinate their operations from Pakistan, and Pakistan, under the pretext of helping the refugees, looks the other way.

On a cold winter evening last December, while on a visit to Peshawar, I talked to two Mujahideen from the Hizb Islami (Army of Islam) faction of the freedom fighters. One of them, a young man in his late 20s, had just returned from Ghazni, about 300 miles southwest of Kabul. They were interested in talking to a fellow Pathan who lives in America. They had come to me with a request for America to supply them with arms.

During our conversation I asked them why they wanted America to give them arms.

"Doesn't America believe in God?" the young man asked.

"Yes, Americans are God-loving people," I replied.

"Don't they know that Russians are nonbelievers?"

"Yes, I think so."

"Then why does not America help us defeat this Roo-Siah [a derogatory term for Russians]? We keep fighting with *golidars* [rifles]; but how long can we fight the helicopters and the tanks?"

"But you must realize that America cannot just jump..."

"Sahib! I know one thing. America sent its big Wazir [meaning chief prime minister-a reference to the visit of former national security adviser Zbigniew Brzezinski last year], who stood at the Khyber pointing a gun at the Hindu Kush mountains and said that he will help us fight the Russians and to go back to our homes and mosques. All believers are supposed to keep their promises. Why didn't he?"

I had no answer.

Tranquility and Turmoil:
Afghans Don't Give Up

Sunday Blade (Behind the News),
December 27, 1984

A simple chain barrier separates Afghanistan from the western border of Pakistan at Torkhum at the fringes of the Khyber Pass.

On each side of the crossing one can see a faint white line painted on the rock cliffs, which for more then a century has constituted the Afghanistan Pakistan boundary.

On a crisp and tranquil morning, members of the paramilitary frontier constabulary went about their chores, while on the other side of the border Afghan guards enjoyed the warm sunshine. An occasional bus, car, or small group of nomads crossed the border.

The tranquility at Torkhum contrasts with the turmoil that this region has been undergoing for five years since the Soviet invasion.

The border line so definite at Torkhum. gives way to a no-man's~land along the 800-mile frontier that three million Afghans have crossed in the last five years and across which small caravans of arms and ammunition are carried to the Afghan heartland.

In many ways the semi-independent communities along the border have never lived in peace. They have fought the Aryans, Alexander the Great, and the Moguls of central Asia on their way to the rich and fertile lands of the Indian subcontinent. When not engaged with invaders, they have fought among themselves.

They paid lip service to the rulers of Afghanistan and India, yet remained fiercely independent and fragmented. Today this remains their greatest asset as well as a terrible liability.

The Soviet Union invaded Afghanistan on December 27, 1979, reportedly with 85,000 soldiers.

The lessons of history apparently were lost upon the rulers in the Kremlin; the four Russian czars had never been able to subjugate Afghanistan. If the modern day weaponry was the Soviets' answer to the fierce independence of the Afghans, it was not to be.

Five years later—despite large-scale military action against the populace, carpet bombing, strafing, destruction of fertile farm land, and the uprooting of more than 3 million people-the Soviet Union remains in a no~win situation.

A ragtag army of freedom fighters—the Mujahideen—has been able to prevent subjugation. The Soviets control the big cities, but most of the countryside remains under the control of the Mujahideen.

Since the start of the conflict, the Mujahideen have been divided into factions along tribal and regional loyalties. Infighting among the groups was as common as their battles against the common enemy.

In recent years, however, a sort of loose alliance has evolved. The bigger of the two alliances is Haft-Gana, or the seven-party alliance, made up of seven fundamentalist religious parties. It is led in strength by the two biggest parties, Hizb Islami (the Army of Islam) and Jamiat Islami (Party of Islam).

They believe in fierce independence from Western as well as Soviet influences.

Their aim of booting the Soviets out of Afghanistan is secondary to the revival and establishment of a social system in keeping with the tenets of Islam.

Thus, resistance to the Soviets is just another facet of their overall struggle started during the rule of King Zahir Shah, years before the Soviet invasion.

Seh-gana, or the three-party alliance, is composed of so-called secular elements—urbane and to an extent westernized technocrats uprooted by the Soviet invasion—whose only mission is to force the Soviets out of Afghanistan.

The religious parties view the three-party secular alliance as wanting to turn the clock back to the times of the king or his successor, Sardar Daud.

The head of the Hizb Islami faction of the seven-party alliance is engineer Gulbadeen Hikmatyar, who has played a major role in uniting the resistance factions. I met him in a nondescript bungalow in the outskirts of Peshawar. We were greeted by his attendants bearing sawed-off machine guns.

Mr. Hikmatyar is an unassuming, gentle, and disarming man in his 40s. In his baggy clothes, turban, and shawl, he could pass for any Pathan tribesman, but his power and influence are felt far beyond Peshawar.

He was an engineering student in the late '50s at Kabul University (hence the honorific "Engineer" used with his name), where he was influenced by the teachings of the Muslim Brotherhood of the Middle East and two professors of religion.

He organized the resistance against the regimes of King Zahir Shah and later Sardar Daud. The rulers of Afghanistan retaliated against the movement and Mr. Hikmatyar went underground.

When the Soviets invaded Afghanistan, Mr. Hikmatyar came to Pakistan to continue his struggle. The former professors—Ustad Abdul Rauf Sayyaf and Ustad Burhanuddin Rabbni—now head the other big factions in the seven-party alliance.

Philosophically they are close to the Akhwanul Muslimeen—the Muslim Brotherhood of the Middle East—and they are unabashed adherents of the writings of the late Syed Qutb, the founder of the brotherhood movement in Egypt, and the late Moulana Maudoudi, the founder of the Jamiat Islami of Pakistan.

Sharing a pot of green tea and biscuits, I inquired about the battle situation on the front.

"This is usually a difficult time of the year for us," Mr. Hikmatyar said. "The Russians take advantage of the cold weather and the bare hills in the countryside to disrupt our movements and supplies. But, by the grace of God, we are coping. The morale of the Mujahideen is high and we are getting used to the hardships."

Are the Russians winning? "If the Russians were winning, then they should have left Afghanistan some time ago," he responded. "In fact, they had planned to stay in Afghanistan not more than a few years.

"According to our estimates, there are about 2.3 million Russians in Afghanistan. Except in the big towns, the Mujahideen control the entire country. Even in Kabul, the Russians cannot roam about alone after dark.

"Anyhow, let's be realistic: We cannot match the Russian weaponry, and at times we have to retreat and hide, but we take back the same ground a few days later."

Mr. Hikmatyar does not like the label "fundamentalist" that the Western press has given him. "We are Muslims and we believe in the teachings of the Koran and the Holy Prophet," he said. "For us, salvation, which includes liberation of Afghanistan, depends upon our faith.

"It is not only the puppet regime of Babrak Karmal and the Russians that have ruined Afghanistan; the Afghan people have been suppressed for a long time, and we wish to restore our just rights to the land.

"Why is it so difficult for other people to see our point of view and our ways?"

An attendant handed Mr. Hikmatyar a slip of paper, which he passed on to me. Scribbled in Pashto, the language common along the border, was amessage: A few days earlier, the Fatah (Victory) Brigade of the Mujahideen had shot down a Soviet MIG fighter plane in the Paktia

111

region.

The alliance is reluctant to talk about its source of military and monetary support, but it does admit to help received from friendly Muslim countries in the Middle East. Most of this aid comes from the West and is channeled through Middle Eastern countries.

Leaders also are sensitive about aligning with the United States. "We do not want Afghanistan to become another Vietnam," Mr. Hikmatyar said. "The Vietnam conflict was between two superpowers. When America pulled out, the Russians took over. We want to be independent of both Russia and America."

The majority of refugees are housed in makeshift camps scattered all along the border inside Pakistan that are under the control of Pakistani officials.

There also are Mujahideen-maintained camps inside Pakistan where freedom fighters recuperate before returning to Afghanistan.

One such camp, established about four years ago, is occupied by 8,000 Mujahideen. It is scattered over the barren foothills of Warsak, about 20 miles outside Peshawar. Nearby is another settlement housing another 6,000 Mujahideen.

Driving by jeep into the guarded Warsak camp, we saw droves of Mujahideen making their way to afternoon prayers in the centrally located mosque, which is spartan but spacious.

Young lads in their teens, young men, and middle-aged men wore baggy clothes, vests, and shawls; they bore no resemblance to the regimented soldiers of a modern-day army. Some bore wounds of recent encounters, while others appeared hearty and robust. They had come from all parts of Afghanistan.

Here are some soldiers we met:

Bakhtiar, an assistant commandant of the camp, in his late 40s, greeted us at his small office-cum-bedroom on a hill. In his ordinary peasant clothes he is a far cry from what we think of as a fighting man.

Sharafat, in his 30s, was just back from Kandooz, the area of Afghanistan adjacent to the Soviet Union. He reported regular artillery shelling and aerial bombardment originating from Soviet territory.

Mirza Muhammad, a field commander, had come from Badakhshan, a region 3 5 days' walk from this camp. Nursing his shattered right arm, he told about the bitter cold, the scarcity of food, and attacks by bandits along the tortuous mountain paths. His men, some bearing open sores on their swollen feet, had been sent back to the front with fresh supplies a few days earlier.

Homemade devices are used with deadly accuracy by the Mujahideen. One field commander told me with great relish of using pressure-cooker bombs against Soviet tanks and convoys. An ordinary pressure cooker with explosives is buried on a country road, and a well-aimed bullet explodes the pot and turns over the passing tank or vehicle.

With a large map of Afghanistan, the fighters pointed to the supply routes and areas of conflict. Looking at the landlocked mountainous country, one wonders how they are able to coordinate their resistance hundreds of miles away inside Afghanistan and even in Kabul.

The Mujahideen have a vast network of informers, many working for the Afghan government and serving in the army. It is because of these informers that the Mujahideen have been able to inflict heavy losses on the Soviet occupiers.

The network is also used to spot spies infiltrating the Mujahideen. When an unidentified refugee arrives in the camp, his story is verified through this network in Afghanistan. Spies and infiltrators are dealt with harshly-reportedly executed, in accordance with tribal codes.

As we were leaving the Warsak camp, a small group of Mujahideen approached the settlement from the mountain range to the west. Exhausted from their long walk, they were greeted and taken to the headquarters office.

A middle-aged man carried a young man piggyback, his leg obviously fractured and immobilized with makeshift wooden splints.

It was a fresh reminder that the conflict is far from over.

Life on the Border: Afghanistan and Pakistan Fight Two Overlapping Wars

Sunday Blade (Behind the News),
March 15, 1992

Nawa Pass
(along the northern frontier of Pakistan and Afghanistan)

A worn-out wire gate strung between two stakes, seldom raised now, demarcates the international border between Pakistan and Afghanistan on this 6,200-foot pass in the Hindu Kush Mountains in northern Pakistan.

Except for the presence of a few Pakistani border militia, this pass could be one of the numerous mountain passes between the two countries. But unlike other passes, Nawa Pass has become the most vital link between Pakistan and the Mujahideen, or the freedom fighters of Afghanistan.

Two wars are being fought among these mountains. One is the 13-year old war for the liberation of Afghanistan, fought inside that nation's borders. The other war, mostly invisible, is being fought on the Pakistani side of the mountains in the Pathan hinterland. This other war is about drugs and smuggling. Sometimes the two overlap.

While there are literally hundreds of passes in these mountains, only a few are wide enough to allow vehicular traffic. The rest are ancient tracks used by pedestrians and pack animals.

Nawa Pass, because of its rather low altitude of 6,200 feet, is open year round. Unlike the Khyber Pass, the most famous of the Hindu Kush passes 60 miles south, Nawa links Pakistan with large areas of Afghanistan that are controlled by the Mujahideen.

The semiautonomous tribes along these mountains have always taken pride in their martial disposition and independent spirit. The British, as others before them who ruled the Indian subcontinent, left the tribes to their own doings as long as they didn't interfere with the policy dictated by the Viceroys of British India.

Many a battle was fought and many legends were created in these mountains, providing fodder for the creative writers of the colonial era. Kipling wrote about such skirmishes in his famous ballad of East and West:

> *Oh, East is East and West is West, and never the twain shall meet,*
> *Till Earth and sky stand presently at God's greatJudgment Seat;*
> *But there is neither East nor West, Border, nor Breed, nor Birth,*
> *When two strong men stand face to face, though they come from*
> *the ends of the earth!*

Pakistan inherited the status quo and the uneasy accommodation with the tribes in 1947 when British India was partitioned into Pakistan and India. The tribes resisted the encroachment of Pakistani authority into their territory, as they had throughout history.

Pakistan kept a military presence in the areas, like the British, to watch the border and to curb any activity detrimental to their interests.

In return, Pakistan continued tribal subsidies and started public health and public works projects. Tribal boys educated in the Pakistani school grew up to hold key positions in public and private sectors, but their reluctance to integrate their areas with the rest of the country continued.

The only worthwhile industry in the tribal areas was the manufacture of small arms and ammunition. In due course, in the 1950s smuggling of consumer goods entered the scene. Goods destined for Afghanistan were unloaded just inside Afghanistan and brought through the mountain passes into tribal territory. Hampered by archaic laws and traditions, Pakistan couldn't do much to curb this traffic. By the late 1970s every Pakistani town along the western frontier could count on an open smuggler's market just a few miles inside the tribal areas.

The Soviet invasion of Afghanistan in 1979 changed the delicate balance. Now a much more important issue dominated the agenda. President Zia of Pakistan gave unconditional support to the Afghan Mujahideen and facilitated the passage of massive U.S. arms to them inside Afghanistan.

Military training camps were set up along the frontier. As the war escalated, three million Afghans uprooted from their homes poured through these passes to reach relative safety on the Pakistani side of the border.

This situation provided unprecedented opportunities for some to increase their involvement in illicit traffic of heroin. With a war going on, nobody had the time or resources to contain the production of powder, as heroin is called in these parts.

From Peshawar, the provincial capital of the Northwest Frontier Province, it takes about 1 1/2 hours to drive a pothole-riddled asphalt road to reach the adjacent northern tribal area of Mohmand Agency, the home of the Mohmand tribe.

The countryside consists of barren hills with scattered stretches of green farmland. There is not much traffic on the road, but the village bazaars along the way are hubs of activity, with frequent traffic jams involving horse-drawn buggies, bicycles, cattle, and small pickup trucks. That is, until one drives through the village of Mian Mandi. Barely a 2-hour drive from Peshawar. The bazaar is devastated. Shops and dwellings have been demolished, some burned to the ground. It is the aftermath of the other war-the drug war.

Poppy has always been grown in these areas on both sides of the mountains. With increased demand for heroin in the West, more and more land was brought under poppy cultivation. Makeshift one-room laboratories sprang up in the tribal areas. The drugs were smuggled out of Pakistan to Europe and then on to North America.

The availability of drugs and arms became so prevalent that in bazaars like Mian Mandi one could see piles of arms displayed in front of shops just as a vendor would display fruits and vegetables. Inside the open shops, opium and its refined product, heroin, were sold openly.

Western countries, especially the United States, leaned heavily upon Pakistan to stop the cultivation of poppy. Pakistan, the recipient of massive military and economic aid in the past ten years, was by this time beginning to have a drug problem of its own.

Pakistan launched a campaign, funded by the United States, to curb poppy cultivation. The tribes and some Afghans, Mujahideen as well as refugees, resisted such efforts, at times with armed confrontations.

A few months ago some officials looking for poppy crops were fired upon. The Pakistani army—in swift reprisal, using heavy artillery—leveled the bazaar. Such skirmishes have been happening with increasing frequency. With such swift reprisals and strong-arm tactics, Pakistan has been able to curb the poppy cultivation to a greater extent. The United States has supplied vehicles and has trained Pakistani field staff to spot and destroy the poppy crops.

Field workers have also been counseling the farmers to grow alternative crops and subsidizing the change. It has put a big dent in the poppy production, but has by no means eliminated it.

Pakistan has no direct control over the poppy fields in Afghanistan. It has, however, influence over the Mujahideen who control the poppy growing areas. Conflicting interests and divergent loyalties produce the inevitable clash of interests. That's where the two wars overlap.

From the devastated village of Mian Mandi, it is another two hours bumpy drive north into the next tribal agency, called Bajaur. A few miles inside Bajaur a road branches off to the west and leads to Nawa Pass. This precarious road, at places no more than a gravel track, snakes up the mountain. Big trucks carrying food, medicine, and arms and bearing Afghan license plates appear too wide and too heavy for this road.

Spent rocket shells, some ten feet long, decorate the mud and wood houses, reminders of a time when the Soviets regularly bombed and shelled these border areas in pursuit of Mujahideen. A small fortress, manned by the Pakistani paramilitary militia, overlooks the beautiful narrow valley from the top of the mountain. Beyond the crest and the wire barrier is Afghanistan.

On the Afghanistan side there is no formal checkpoint. A roadside tent a hundred yards beyond the barrier gives some semblance of a checkpoint. A small sign proclaims the territory under the control of the *Hizb-i-Islami* (Army of Islam) faction of the Mujahideen.

Spent rocket shells and a rusting Soviet armored personnel carrier are the only signs that this beautiful valley and the country beyond are still in the grips of a long civil war.

Mujahideen control most of the Afghan countryside, like this valley, whereas the Kabul regime controls the major cities and surrounding areas. With the cessation of U.S. military aid to the Mujahideen, their dream of marching into Kabul looks progressively distant.

The Kabul regime of Najibullah has proven resilient, and even though the former Soviet Union, in agreement with the United States, stopped aid to Kabul, the regime has managed to survive. A negotiated settlement between Pakistan, Mujahideen, and the Kabul government is being brokered by the United Nations.

Pakistan, until recently a champion of military victory, now realizes the futility of an ongoing war which has put enormous political and economic pressure on her. With three million restless refugees within its border, Pakistan can ill afford to continue to be a party to an open-ended, drawn-out conflict.

This compromise has caused bitterness among some of the more militant factions of the Mujahideen, who would not settle for anything less than an all-out victory—a victory that, under the present circumstances, looks most unlikely.

Pakistan has another pressing reason to have this conflict resolved. With the breakup of the Soviet Union, the newly independent central Asian states would like to reestablish the trade routes which existed between the subcontinent and central Asia as far back as recorded history.

On their way from Tashkent to Peshawar those caravans passed through Afghanistan. Ongoing conflict in Afghanistan precludes resumption of any trade between Pakistan and the newly independent central Asian republics.

From the crest of the mountains and beyond the wire barrier of Nawa Pass, the Kunar Valley of Afghanistan is like a picture postcard. With the backdrop of snow-capped mountains in the distance, the Kunar River meanders through the fertile landscape. From this height one cannot see the devastation that this 13-year-old war has brought to this land. People have settled into an uneasy accommodation with events over which they have no control. Refugees continue to live in the camps in Pakistan, hoping to return to their homes some day.

Farmers grow poppies on the mountainsides, and somewhere in the tribal areas in makeshift laboratories opium is turned into heroin. Arms and ammunition trickle into the Afghan countryside through these passes, at places carried by American-supplied mules, to engage an enemy that has become formidable.

In the meantime the drug barons get richer and a few more youths in Lahore or Karachi or Amsterdam get hooked. In these intertwining and overlapping wars, it seems there are very few winners.

The Flood of Afghan Refugees Hurts
the Local Peshawar Population

Sunday Blade (Behind the News), July 12, 1992

The mere mention of Peshawar in a bygone era evoked memories of an enchanting town located on the caravan route of central Asia. Like the fabled cities of Samarkand, Tashkent, Balkh, Bukhara, and Kabul, Peshawar was an important stop for the trade caravans traveling from central Asia to the Indian subcontinent and beyond.

Today this ancient city in the foothills of the Khyber Mountains is a sad reminder of its glorious past. Overpopulation, urban decay, and over 5 years of civil war just across the border in Afghanistan have taken a toll that no other city in Pakistan has suffered.

Peshawar was the first stop on this route when the caravans crossed the Hindu Kush Mountains. It beckoned weary travelers after an arduous journey through those mountains.

In its bazaars and inns people from all corners of the world rubbed shoulders and bartered goods. They unwound in the tea shops in the labyrinthine alleys of the old city and listened to the professional storytellers telling imaginary as well as real accounts, often exaggerated, of past events.

It was this strategic location, as well as the promise of riches in the Indian subcontinent, which compelled many invaders to venture into the Peshawar Valley. Most, like the Persians and Alexander in the era before the birth of Christ, returned home. Some, like the Moguls in the 17th century, stayed and established dynasties.

The British were the last of the invaders to enter the Peshawar valley, in the mid 19th century, to establish their control. Peshawar did not match the splendor and opulence of the other cities of the subcontinent-like Delhi, Bombay, and Jaipur—but it was a frontier town, still wild and unpredictable, and it caught the imagination of the British.

It became the farthest outpost of the British Raj. It was here in the Pathan hinterland that many battles were fought and legends created which provided fodder for writers like Kipling, Churchill, and others of the colonial era.

In 1947, when the British gave independence to the Indian subcontinent, that change resulted in the creation of Pakistan. Refugees from India crossed the new border into Pakistan, and many of them made their way to Peshawar.

At the time Peshawar had a population of 100,000. With the influx of so many refugees from India, as well as the migration of frontier nomads to the area, the city grew, and by the mid-1970s it had a population of 250,000. Civic amenities were able, with difficulty, to keep pace with the population growth.

The city managed. The water carriers sprinkled the streets in the summer afternoon to settle the dust, and sweepers with long brooms swept the roads and streets. The open sewers flowed unimpeded. Fresh water was in abundant supply, and the public parks and gardens were well maintained. A walk through the narrow alleys of the old town made one's heart glad by the sight of hanging flower baskets from the second floor windows of the old houses.

And then hell broke loose.

The Soviet Union invaded Afghanistan in December of 1979. In the ensuing fierce and brutal struggle, one-fourth of the population of Afghanistan became homeless. They poured down through the mountain passes into Pakistan and made their way to the nearest population centers along the frontier.

Four million refugees entered Pakistan—a staggering 3 million around Peshawar, and the rest along the 1,500-mile-long border between the two countries.

Pakistanis, despite their own economic woes, opened their hearts to help their Muslim brethren, as did international relief agencies. The refugees were provided with cash stipends, food, clothing, and shelter.

Although most of the refugees registered with the Pakistani government, many did not. These Afghans, because of a common language and religion, became part of the local scene. The well-to-do bought properties and businesses and slowly worked their way into the area economy. The registered refugees ran small businesses and competed for construction and day laborer jobs with the local population, edging them out by offering to work for lower wages.

Early one morning, while passing in the city center, one could see about 50 laborers, with their shovels, picks, and paintbrushes, sitting on the side of the street near the clock tower, waiting for the contractor to hire them as day laborers. Not a single one was a local laborer.

The Afghans also bought local property in record numbers, thus driving real estate prices beyond the reach of ordinary citizens.

With the outsiders outnumbering the natives, the cultural and social changes have been profound and perhaps everlasting. Although in the beginning of the Afghan conflict there was a feeling of obligation toward the guests, their prolonged presence spawned hostility and resentment.

This also reflects the fact that the Pakistanis blame Afghans for the increasing menace of illegal trafficking of heroin and arms. While in the past drugs were exported to the West, now the problem has also affected the local population.

Government policy dictates that despite the resentment and unhappiness of the local population, a pleasant and cheerful front has to be maintained, even though their own people have been pushed to the bottom.

Government officials are cautiously optimistic that once a semblance of political stability returns to Afghanistan the refugees will return to their homeland. However, many in the government concede that about 15 to

20 percent of the refugees will somehow stay in Pakistan.

In Peshawar the transportation, currency market, rug trade, and many other lucrative businesses are owned or controlled by Afghans. For them to leave successful businesses for an uncertain future in Afghanistan is tantamount to economic suicide.

In the short as well as the long run, the demographics of Peshawar will be in favor of the foreigners. By any stretch of the imagination, the stay of refugees in Pakistan for more than 15 years and the eventual absorption of so many of them into Pakistani society is unprecedented.

Pakistan was forced to do this despite its own precarious economic condition. Added to this burden is the recent cutoff by the United States of all economic aid to Pakistan.

The United Nations and the Pakistani government have a plan to repatriate the refugees back to Afghanistan in an orderly manner. There is talk of large-scale international efforts to rebuild the devastated country. Unfortunately, most of such proposals are meant for Afghanistan only. No one has talked about helping the frontier areas of Pakistan, some of which have suffered as much as Afghanistan, if not more. Such help is paramount in the minds of the local people like Mazhar Ali Shah.

Mr. Shah is a high-ranking officer in the provincial government who administers the tribal areas of Mohmand, located between Pakistan and Afghanistan. He reckons that this new wave of foreigners will drown the indigenous population of Peshawar to the point where, in the next few generations, it will be hard to find people who speak the local language or adhere to the centuries-old customs.

Peshawar appears prosperous and booming. The bazaars and markets hum with commercial activity. The rich and the affluent, Pakistanis as well as Afghans, live in beautiful mansions with marble facades in new satellite towns around Peshawar. They are the beneficiaries of the artificial prosperity created by the war in Afghanistan. Pushed to the bottom of the heap and forgotten are the local people who, through no fault of

their own, have become strangers in their homeland and have lost out to
the refugees from Afghanistan.

Islamic Dream Still
Unfulfilled for Freedom Fighters

Sunday Blade (Behind the News Section),
November 3, 1993

They were the idealistic young men from all over the Middle East and the world who responded when a call came for Jihad, or holy war. After the end of the war, they were shunned, and were called fundamentalists and even terrorists. They are the young Arab and some non-Arab men who, having fought in Afghanistan, now find themselves unwelcome, living in a foreign country.

When the former Soviet Union invaded Afghanistan in 1979, the Afghans rose in a popular rebellion to wage a protracted guerrilla war against the superpower. This struggle for liberation against an avowed atheist regime caught the imagination of many Muslim youths around the world. Living under autocratic and often brutal regimes, these deeply religious young men found the struggle in Afghanistan most appealing. Here an infidel country had occupied an Islamic state. The populace had risen to get rid of the invaders and to bring in an Islamic order.

The neighboring Muslim country of Pakistan had opened its doors to receive displaced Afghan refugees and provided much-needed sanctuary for the Afghan fighters.

Most Arab countries, from Algeria to the Gulf, made it easy for their young men to join the Jihad. For some, it was an easy way to get rid of some deeply religious and potentially troublesome young men.

These countries were mindful of the activities of various Islamic organizations in the Middle East trying to bring about a new Islamic order. As a result, the Pakistani frontier town of Peshawar, just across the Afghanistan border in the foothills of the Khyber mountains, became the cherished destination for some of these young men.

They came from many countries. Many came from Western countries

126

like the United States, Canada, and Britain. The Islamic movement the world over glamorized the Afghan struggle and encouraged these young men—many of them college students and young professionals—to put their lives on hold and participate in the Jihad.

They were issued papers, given aliases (to shield them from the ever vigilant spies from different Middle Eastern countries), and assigned to refugee camps scattered along the Pakistani side of the border.

Once their credibility and sincerity were established, they were given military training under the supervision of one of the Mujahideen factions.

After the withdrawal of Soviet forces in 1990 and the subsequent fall of the communist regime in Kabul two years later, most of the young Arabs and non-Arabs returned to their homelands.

However, a sizable number, perhaps in the hundreds, remain in Peshawar and Afghanistan. A majority of them are associated with nongovernmental organizations, called NGOs, providing humanitarian and rehabilitative service to the Afghans.

Whereas most Western NGOs either left or were obliged to leave Pakistan at the end of the war, the Arab NGOs continue to provide much needed assistance to the Afghans.

It is estimated that through the duration of the conflict these Arab NGOs provided half a billion dollars worth of aid to Afghanistan, a sum greater than all of the Western and Afghan NGOs combined.

Most of the Arab and Muslim NGOs are funded privately and are committed to humanitarian efforts such as running hospitals, staffing basic health facilities, schools, orphanages, religious centers, and providing potable water. But according to informed sources, there are a few NGOs that are still running training camps in Afghanistan.

Since most of their activities are under the auspices of one of the various

Mujahideen factions, it is difficult to tell if such camps are for Afghan Mujahideen or for training non-Afghans.

The young men represent a religious-political spectrum from the far right to the center.

The former believe in the most pristine form of religion and hence are quite unwilling to compromise on such subjects as secular democracy, rights of women, modern arts, or a meaningful dialogue with anyone who holds a different view.

Those on the other end of the spectrum show some flexibility, if only to achieve their ultimate goal of an Islamic order deeply rooted in the teachings of the Koran and the Prophet Muhammad.

Arab countries mindful of these orthodox young men have reacted differently to their presence in Pakistan. Saudi Arabia has lured many of its young men back by offering them lucrative jobs. Some countries, like the Gulf States, have remained oblivious. Still others, like Egypt, linking at least some of them to anti-state terrorist activities in Egypt, want them returned.

Pressure from Egypt and the United States led Pakistani authorities to round up all such Arab nationals in Peshawar a few months ago. Most of them, to the embarrassment of the Pakistani officials, had legitimate reasons and appropriate documents to be in Pakistan. Therefore, the courts set them free.

But the doubts linger. Their cause was not helped when the now-imprisoned preacher, Shaikh Omar Abdul Rahman, had opted to go to Afghanistan instead of Egypt, his native country, when he was threatened with expulsion from the United States.

Some of the young men have decided to settle down in Pakistan, and have married or brought their families to Peshawar.

Unfortunately, the Pakistani religious parties and the Afghan Mujahideen groups—their previous supporters—have not come to their defense as strongly as they could have.

For many young Arab (and non-Arab) Muslims who have returned to their home countries, the Afghan experience has been uplifting and positive. But for many others, who either stayed back or have since returned to Peshawar, the aftermath has been frustrating.

While they participate in the struggle to rebuild Afghanistan, their cherished goal of an ideal Islamic order for the Muslim world remains distant and elusive.

Glossary

Afghan: one who is from Afghanistan; in British colonial era the term was used loosely to describe all Pushtuns living on both sides of the Indo-afghan border.

Al-Qaeda: literally the way or method; a social and welfare organization established in the early 90's for Arab veterans of the Afghan war; over time it became a vehicle for terrorist activities with world-wide reach.

Amir-ul-Momineen: commander of the faithful; a title used by the caliphs in early Islamic history

Arab-Afghans: mercenaries from Arab and Muslim countries who fought the Soviets along the side of Afghan Mujahideen; many of them stayed back and became part of Bin Laden's Al-Qaeda organization

alim: religious scholar; pleural ulema

buz kashi: ancient game of horsemanship where rival teams try to snatch a goat carcass and carry it to the goal post.

dari: Afghan version of Persian language

Deobandi: after the city of Deoband in India; those who follow the religious interpretations of the original madrassa established in the middle of the 19th century

Durand Line: after Sir Mortimer Durand; the boundary between Afghanistan and British India (now Pakistan) demarcated in 1893

Durrani: a Pushtun tribe; most of the Afghan kings came from Durrani tribe

fatwa: formal religious edict; religious opinion or declaration by the ulema

Gandhara: King Kanishka's kingdom in the first century AD that comprised the present day Afghanistan, Pakistan and adjacent areas of India

Ghilzai: a pushtun tribe; stronghold of top Taliban leadership

hadith: recorded sayings of the Prophet

Hazara: a shia tribe from northwest of Afghanistan

hijab: head covering or veil worn by some Muslim women in public

ijtihad: independent reasoning in interpretation of Islamic law; intrpretation of religion according to times; innovation within Islamic law

imam: a person who leads the congregation in prayers; a leader

Islam: submission or surrender to the will of God; surrender to peace

jihad: struggle; striving spiritually or physically against evil either within oneself or against an enemy

kafir: non believer; one who does not believe in God

Loya Jirga: grand assembly of tribal elders; an old Afghan institution

madrassa: religious school, college or seminary

mahram: a close male relative that must accompany a woman outside the home

Mujahid (pl. mujahideen): holy freedom fighter; soldier of God *mullah*: one who takes care of the mosque and lead the congregation in prayers; honorific for graduates of madrassas

Muslim: from Islam; one who submits to the will of God

Pushtu or Pukhtu: language spoken by the Pushtuns

Pushtun or Pukhtun: tribes in the south and southwest of Afghanistan and along the western frontier of Pakistan

Quran: collection of revelations that God revealed to Prophet Muhammad over a period of 23 years

Ramadan: the Muslim month of fasting

serai: an inn along the old caravan routes

shalwar-kameez: baggy pants and long shirt worn in Afghanistan and Pakistan

sharia: law based on the Quran and the sunnah-the traditions of the Prophet; literally: the path to be followed

shia: Those Muslims who believe that Ali the cousin and son-in-law of the Prophet was true inheritor of the Prophet's legacy and therefore should have become the first caliph upon the Prophet's death

shura: consultative body

sunnah: customs, sayings and traditions of the Prophet

sunni: literally: those who follow sunnah; majority Muslims sect

Tajik: one of the largest non-Pushtun tribes from north of Afghanistan

taqlid: literally: to follow; to imitate; to accept the traditional interpretation of religion

ummah: a community of faithful; generally the world-wide community of Muslims

Uzbek: one of the northern Afghan tribes

Wahhabism*:* an Islamic revival movement started in Saudi Arabia in the 19th century

Index

135